CONTENTS

Introduction

A Spirituality of Self-Esteem

They never failed to move him, those golden windows in the house on the hill. Regularly, after supper, the boy would look across the valley and his eyes would sparkle as he wondered at the beauty that stirred him so deeply. One evening, drawn toward the light, he felt compelled, with the setting of the sun, to follow his heart's allurement. It would be a long journey down into the dark valley where the wild things wandered and then the dangerous climb up the rocky hill-face to the house with the windows of wonder.

There was a strange silence and many shifting shadows as the small hero pressed forward, trusting his instincts to guide him through the night. He learned, as he journeyed on, to befriend the darkness, to accept the pain of his lostness, and to believe in the power of the light that he loved. As dawn breaks, the young adventurer is scratched and bruised, now climbing slowly, but approaching with every step the object of his desire and admiration.

Breathless with excitement but spent from his long night's adventures the boy collapses wearily on the doorstep. "Please tell me," he whispers to the bright-eyed woman who extends her arms to him, "is this the house with the golden windows?" With a smile she shakes her head. Her eyes are full of compassion. There is concern too in her voice. Will the boy understand her truth? She is pointing back over the valley still shrouded in mist and shadow. High on the hill was a little house, its windows on fire with the pure white light of the morning sun. Quietly they stood in the presence of mystery. The boy sensed it was the most important moment of his life. "There," the woman gently said, "there where you live you will find the windows of wonder."

It is so easy to become separated from one's true heart. Not all of us find it as early as the boy in the story. But it is never too late to rediscover our most beautiful and trustworthy center, to rejoice in our recovered power, to sense the mystery that beckons us in. Our hearts are made for wonder and love but today they are undernourished. We are born for true beauty but we pursue illusions. Our spirits thirst for truth in a land of lies.

We search for ways to follow our bliss. We long to look through windows of wonder into the love and meaning at the heart of creation. We yearn to be convinced of our own worth and value, especially when powerful forces persuade us otherwise. What will sustain us on our nighttime journey of pain through the valley where the wild things are, in quest of the wise counselor? Where do we find the bread and wine to nourish our hope? What will end the famine of our hearts? Only the stories of life.

Our hearts are starved of stories—stories about our infancy in the womb of God twenty billion years ago, about the grace that powers the cosmos into its mysterious future, about the unforgettable wedding night when the divine-human love-marriage changed the world; stories about befriending pain and transforming its power, about dreaming the darkness into creative light. These are healing stories, fresh and green, for disillusioned souls. They whisper to the imagination. They call up the sleeping mystic and artist within us. Without such tales nothing is young anymore. And these are the oldest stories in the world. In fact God told the first one. He told it with infinite love. We are that story. How did we ever forget it?

"Creation spirituality" is the name I give to the basic collection of stories about our human beauty. This book is written for those who have not heard the story, so that forevermore it will continue to be written on our sacred human hearts. It is divided into four parts or windows—the four paths of creation spirituality. These represent the wonder, the darkness, the healing and the transformation in evolving creation and in growing human love. Each of the sixteen sub-themes is presented in light of the fresh and exciting insights that the mystical tradition brings to a sometimes colorless and rather gloomy set of beliefs and practices. Countless numbers of jaded spirits are healing, growing and rejoicing in the compassion and justice of this redis-covered story as a new love and meaning are revealed at the heart of a world filled with pain and beauty.

A creation-centered spirituality of the heart always inspires a more confident, balanced and optimistic sense of self-value and self-worth. At a time in the history of the world when self-esteem seems to be a rare pearl of great price, it seems ap-propriate to offer a spirituality that affirms the love and beauty and meaning in all creation but especially in the human heart. The mighty lover, artist and healer that live within us are hungry for the great but forgotten stories that nurture the imag-ination. The mystic, prophet and contemplative that hide in our unused inner rooms are, in fact, old friends of creation spirituality. They long to be reintroduced.

Each reading is an attempt to reclaim some aspect of a lost tradition, to rediscover another way of apprehending the mys-tery of our lives; it offers a challenge to the reader to transcend dualistic thinking and to explore the mystery of God's uncondi-tional compassion. I sincerely hope that these stories and your story will meet and dance to a fresh and liberating rhythm. They will then become windows of wonder to enchant and bless your children.

First Window

The Wonder of You

ACCEPTANCE

The Way To Blossom

The boy who lived in the house with the golden windows came to understand that he had already within himself all that he sought outside. The windows of wonder are for looking in to the rich mystery of our own spirit and on to the flow of being of which it is a part. Our self-esteem is secured, not by searching for another work of art, but by bringing the work of art that we already are closer to the window; our self-acceptance is deepened by turning up the volume on the music that we can already faintly hear within us, not by lusting after another score.

In this first reflection I want to draw attention to the importance of self-acceptance and to some of the reasons for embracing this fundamental attitude. My reason for this is based on the conviction that we are fine as we are and often lose whatever peace we have by pursuing unrealistic goals. The person you essentially are now is the surest basis for self-esteem, not the person you might become. The "wonder of you" springs from the mystery of your existence at this very moment, not from a "new you" tomorrow. In other words, our time might be better spent in exploring and realizing who we already are than in striving to change ourselves into some kind of "super-self," or, as a University of Pennsylvania psychologist recently put it, "into the California self."

Please bear with me while I try to make myself clear. There

is something basically simple that needs to be said. It seems to me that there is one elemental, infinite flow of energy permeating all creation. This is the source of life. It sweeps through the tiniest particle, it sustains the mighty cosmos. It has its own timing, yet it is beyond time. It has no name; it has a million names. It is generally perceived as a benign power, a loving creative force.

Now to a greater or lesser extent we humans are part of that flow. Most of us accept that this is so. We are aware that we belong to something greater than ourselves. We sense that our completion, salvation and liberation are achieved by greater intimacy with the infinite energy that holds everything together —an energy now acknowledged by almost all "respectable" secular sciences. What I wish to attempt in this opening section is to offer one outline of the interrelatedness between our own personal being and becoming on the one hand and that divine compassion on the other. My aim in doing this is to suggest that, once we become aware of the wonder of that intimacy, the path toward spiritual freedom, transcendence, enlightenment, or whatever we want to call it lies in the acceptance of ourselves, of our relatedness with others, of our roles as part of a whole, rather than in the development of a "new self," an autonomous fulfillment, a "doing your own thing" that often comes across as a lonely, rather selfish preoccupation devoid of social compassion. It is not that I'm ambivalent about the utter necessity for change and growth, for searching and transcending; it is simply that inner awareness and self-acceptance, in my opinion, hold the key to all we desire. The desire to change, to "do your own thing," may spring from desperation and frustration; it may be sustained by a form of violence that is destructive and introspective.

We seek to change in order to be accepted, to conform to expectations, to live up to the ideal image we have made up for ourselves. We are impatient with ourselves, and so we want to force ourselves to change. But no growth ever results from violence. The only growth-promoting change is that which comes from self-acceptance. Change can never be forced; it occurs. Resistance to ourselves, to anything in ourselves, only serves to strengthen that which we are resisting, and thus makes change impossible.[1]

According to Anthony de Mello, acceptance of reality does not in any way mean conformism, passivity, apathy or inertia. It is a joyful recognition of the all that is, in order to make the best of things as they are and of life as it is. Setting off on one's own to change oneself is, at best, a waste of time, at worst, a cause for bitter disillusion. "In a straight line, nobody goes very far," mused the Little Prince. Recognition of reality, acceptance and awareness of the mystery that we already are, in no way invite complacency but provide the vision and tactics for personal growth and social transformation. In our acceptance of reality we become acutely aware of the interrelatedness of all creatures, of our dependency on each other, on our need to love and be loved so that self-esteem and confidence may grow. Only in relationship, not alone, do we blossom. Susan Griffin wrote, "We can pull the grass free of the earth and see its separate roots—but when the grass is free, it dies."[2]

Any consideration of self-acceptance must face the fact of our weakness, woundedness and incompleteness. It is here precisely that the principle of acceptance as growth-inducing is most convincing. It is at the point of imperfection that development happens. The imperfection in the crystal, for instance, is perfectly placed for further growth—only there can change take place. The only place that further evolution is possible is where the incompleteness is revealed and accepted. Very often the peace of mind we seek is achieved not so much by filling in the gaps and correcting the flaws in our personalities and capacities but in understanding them accurately and then accepting them as part of reality. This rich insight into our own wound-edness is already a healing experience. Because all being, all creation and life, is the incarnation and child of love itself, it can be trusted to bring about what is best for universal harmony. Given half a chance, the flow of cosmic power, the great under-ground river of the mystics, will transform the imperfect toward wholeness. Thus is the raw courage of those who dare to face their wounds and accept them rewarded.

To savor the flavor of the excitement of being is one of the first results of self-acceptance. We are empowered to achieve this, and it is a rare grace. In the very acceptance of our exis-tence we are drawn outside it. Matthew Fox reminds us that the great Thomas Aquinas, the touchstone of Roman Catholic orthodoxy, held that every human person is *capax universi*—ca-pable of the universe. He is inviting every human person to a cosmic awakening, a cosmic relationship.[3] And what do we see when we look into the world of mystery, into this sacred place which is sustained by God's grace? We sense that we are in the presence of the being to whom we are allured. We feel a closer bonding with the beauty of which we are already a part. We know a greater intimacy with the love that we as Christians call God. This vision and consequent growth in being and becom-ing is already implicit in self-acceptance.

This kind of vision comes slowly and usually with some pain. The way to it is the way of "letting go," of stripping away everything down to the self. Only then does the truth reveal itself. The danger in so many "instant vision" approaches ad-vertised today is that they have no permanence. There is, how-ever, no fake authenticity! Beauty reveals itself slowly and usually in the ordinary events and moments of life. The key to God lies in a new way of perceiving the ordinary rather than in looking for the extraordinary. While partaking in expensive crash courses to build our self-esteem by affirming our power to change and our right to happiness, we can often miss the object of our desire pressing in on us from all sides every day wherever we happen to be. "Does the fish soar to find the ocean, the eagle plunge to find the air?" Our condition of blind searching out there for what is already within and around us is as contradictory as the notion of a thirsty fish in the sea or a flying bird seeking air.

The open secret lies in the fact that we are children of love and beauty, sustained and surrounded by these divine graces. Why then do we seek to change? And what precisely do we want to change? What is needed is a clearer vision of who we already are, sharper focus on what is already there. By shifting unnecessary baggage from our backs we can stand straighter for a better perspective. By letting go of misleading and confusing information about creation, incarnation and destiny, poured into us when we were impressionable and vulnerable, we clear the air and bare our hearts for keener perception and awareness. We then gladly accept and trust those same hearts to draw us unerringly along the path of love and beauty for which we were carefully designed and coded. Put in another way, the task for the gutsy reader of this book is not so much to find a guru or saint who will reveal the way to the garden of bliss; neither is it to become such a special person by acquiring new knowledge and revelations; it is rather to identify, befriend and set free the mystic within, the child of intense compassion and wisdom already deeply in love with you, who is aching to be trusted as your true and divine self.

This is not the place to outline the incarnational theology or the creational spirituality that underpin the panentheism advocated in this section. It may be sufficient at this stage merely to reassure the reader of the Christian orthodoxy of my convictions about the immanence and indwelling of the Holy Spirit, or, as the traditional catechism put it in Q.3, "Where is God?" to which we all replied "God is everywhere." The suggestions in this book about waiting, letting go, centering, living in the "now," are offered as paths to a deeper awareness of the wonder that we are—both creation in general and ourselves in particular—and then to a glad acceptance of ourselves as unique and sacred. "In music, in the sea, in a flower, in a leaf, in an act of kindness; I see what people call God in all these things," wrote Pablo Casals. And St. Paul reminds us that in him we live and move and have our being.

Since we are dealing here with immense issues to do with fundamental options for life, basic attitudes toward the pursuit of happiness, understanding the presence of the divine in our midst, listening to our own stammering hearts—since we are, in fact, exploring the edges of sheer mystery, our best approach is to settle for glimpses of meaning, little windows of wonder here and there that open and shut in surprising ways, vignettes of beauty that console and reassure, encouraging us in our trusting and risking. The kind of self-acceptance we are considering here is facilitated not so much by an accumulation of information and knowledge about this or that, but by a readiness for the sudden moments of disclosure when the bright shining, that is already and always everywhere, is momentarily unveiled before our startled eyes.

This book is about such moments. I wish to finish this section with a reminder about the intimate interplay of love between God, the universe and our own hearts. Dylan Thomas refers to this intrinsic relationship when he writes:

> The force that through the green fuse drives the flower
> Drives my green age . . .
> The force that drives the water through the rocks
> Drives my red blood.[4]

Thomas Berry, director of the Riverdale Center for Religious Research in New York City, is a prophet of our times. His warnings about the unprecedented destruction and wanton desecration of the natural world by the human species are sending shock waves throughout ever-widening circles of concerned environmentalists. In the course of one such warning he describes with characteristic insight the delicate network of interdependence between the divine presence in nature and our human spirit. Reverent self-acceptance includes the acknowledgment of finely balanced spiritual interconnections. But careless exploitation has cosmic repercussions.

> We should be clear about what happens when we destroy the living forms of this planet. The first consequence is that we destroy modes of Divine presence. If we have a wonderful sense of the Divine, it is because we live amid such awesome magnificence. If we have refinement of emotion and sensitivity, it is because of the delicacy, the fragrance, and indescribable beauty of soul and of music and of rhythmic movement in the world about us. If we grow in our life vigor, it is because the earthly community challenges us, forces us to struggle to survive, but, in the end, reveals itself as a benign providence. But, however benign, it must provide that absorptive drama of existence whereby we can experience the thrill of being alive in a fascinating and unending sequence of adventures.[5]

Our humanity is interwoven with everything in the universe. In self-acceptance we adopt a whole new family of relations. To be free to accept we must let go of many preoccupations. This freedom brings a keen awareness of our true beauty. And the transformation is under way. "Speak to us of God," the cherry tree was asked. And the cherry tree blossomed.

AWARENESS

Waking the Mystic

Creation spirituality is about coming alive. The mystic in each of us may be sleeping. Awareness has to do with inner listening and inner vision. Images abound concerning the awakening of our potential to be present to and interact with the rest of creation. Sometimes the flash of vision is sudden and deep, a moment of inner insight that illuminates and clarifies. Again the image may be that of joining a flowing source of creative imagination. This is a favorite image in the mystical tradition where God is likened to a great underground river and well-spring of inspiration. These images help us to intensify the link between attention and understanding, between knowledge and wisdom, between perception and love.

When our inner mystic wakes up there is an awareness that we are no longer as separate as we ordinarily take ourselves to be: that under certain circumstances we may become directly and intuitively aware of our oneness with others and with the universe in a deeply moving manner. Monica Furlong writes:

> I was waiting at a bus stop on a wet afternoon. It was oppo-
> site the Odeon cinema, outside the station, and I was
> surrounded by people, shops, cars. A friend was with me.
> All of a sudden, for no apparent reason, everything looked

different. Everything I could see shone, vibrated, throbbed with joy and with meaning. I knew that it had done this all along, and would go on doing it, but that usually I could not see it. I was aware of being regarded by love, of being wholly accepted. . . . It was all over in a minute or two. I climbed on to the bus, saying nothing to my friend—it seemed impossible to explain—and sat stunned with astonishment and happiness.[6]

I have collected many such testimonies to the hidden wonder of our surroundings. So has Edward Robinson of the Religious Experience Research Unit in Oxford, England:

There was yet another feeling that used to come to me which now I can only call a kind of insight. At the time, when I was a child, I only remember the feeling as one of intense reality and knowing, a sort of grown-up feeling when I really saw and knew how things really were underneath appearances. At these times of knowing I did not see colors, nor hear strange hums; but rather saw the ordinary world very clearly and in infinite details, and knew it to be all joined up, and all made of one primal substance or life-force which whipped up the poles of duality. I could see how we are all one substance and interdependent, and all joined, and how in reality nothing has a fixed immovable edge or skin, but all things merge into their surroundings. This kind of insight took place in the deepest part of me. . . . I understood without seeing. . . .[7]

The desire toward intimacy is powerful beyond description, and when even partially achieved it is convinced of the limitlessness of the soul's potential for growth and unity. It is only when our awareness is finely tuned that this desire can begin to be fulfilled. And this fine-tuning comes only with the discipline of eternal vigilance. Creation-centered awareness is about seeing what is already there. It is in silence that this is achieved. The faster and more strenuous the travel, the more blurred the vision. What is to be achieved is an unforced attentiveness. All strain is counter-productive. When we let go the anxiety that preoccupies the heart we begin to see into the mystery of things. We miss less beauty. "Only that day dawns," wrote Thoreau, "to which we are awake." Such days are lovely days, filled with wonder and worship.

There is an Indian greeting that establishes the new guest as a visiting deity. In the best Christian tradition this vision is also insisted upon. Only through prayer and fasting can such an awareness be maintained. There are many lapses. One evening several months ago I was writing a poem called "Incognito." It was about the God who always surprises us in the variety and unpredictability of his visits among us. The fourth verse advised vigilant awareness of incarnate divinity wherever the anawim were gathered in their poverty, their wounds, their handicaps. At this point there was a loud knocking at the door. Impatiently I opened it to find "old Mick" back yet again for more hand-outs, going through his litany of misfortunes and desperate needs. Cutting him short, I reminded him of my impressive extravagance to him a few days previously. He was abusing my generosity and I rather stridently ordered him out of the building. His expectant eyes clouded over and, stooped with daily humiliation, he shambled off. Back at my desk the penny dropped . . . and dropped . . . Once again I had been living in my head and had failed to notify my sleeping heart. It was an ungracious moment. I was neither balanced nor awake. But my painful and acute realization of this was also a blessed moment of disclosure. I had lost my center. I want to devote the remainder of this reflection on awareness to the place and importance of "centering" in our lives.

Centering is about homecoming. There is a place within that we always recognize in a new way. It is a center of quietness where we are known and held; a center where we stop pretending, where we are free to be ourselves. It is the masks that unbalance us. We overreach to achieve unnecessary goals, we are caged in by the expectations of others, programmed by institutional agendas, limited and bounded by closed systems of belief and social doctrines. But the centered spirit carries its center of gravity lightly wherever it goes: it drops and draws its anchor as it pleases. Its power and symmetry come directly from the source, unfiltered by awkward human structures and often clumsy institutions. The centered spirit draws its vision and power straight from the springs of divine, creative love.

Centering and recentering require trust. Our distractions, our compulsive sense of duty and our workaholic anxiety about profitable use of time, keep us off center and off balance. Our emotions become unpredictable, our attitudes inappropriate. The homing device in our hearts gets interfered with. And they stray in confusion. But we know when we are moving toward the light. It is like second nature. We sense the right direction. We trust our hearts. They are coded for travel on the beam of bliss. There is a Navajo story about the pollen path. Pollen is the life-source. The pollen path is the path to the center. Are you on the pollen path? Am I?

As I sat down to continue my writing one hour ago I accidentally wiped out this whole section on centering. I was explaining the miracle of word-processing to a friend and in a careless moment pressed the wrong key. A whole day's work of particularly demanding material disappeared irretrievably in a split second. I fumed and raged inwardly. I wanted to blame and accuse. My pathetic overreaction could be called a tantrum—a rather sorry spectacle for my friend who kept a much-needed sense of perspective throughout the whole affair. The ironic aspect of the sad little interlude was that the lost material was about centering—what you are reading now being my second attempt! Ironic, because of the credibility gap between my words of wisdom to my readers and my personal little sulk and panic at a very insignificant and inconsequential incident. The odds were that the cosmos would survive the losses. You will be glad to know that I regulated my breathing, did a few exercises, reflected on what I had written about calmness and balance and gradually returned from outside the periphery back to the center. Having removed all sharp objects from my room, my friend hurried home.

While we cannot do much to avoid the initial impact of our emotions as we react to what comes suddenly, there is much we can do to center ourselves again as soon as possible. Ideally we would hope to remain centered in all circumstances. That aim is what this book is about. How do I avoid a repetition of that graceless encounter with my traveling friend Michael? How do we keep grace under pressure? How are we convinced of our own beauty? Is it possible to live unencumbered by baggage? When will I dance between the light and the shadow, moving without fear to the different beats? What must I *do* to become centered?

"In the beginning was the dream and the dream was with God and the dream was God." How do we live God's dream for us? God's dream is like a great underground river that calls us to its heart. When we go with its flow we are centered. But we must let go before we dive into it, unlearn so much before we swim. Our place is in the water, not on the river bank. God is already at our center. Centering is more about letting go of the wrong maps than about drawing new ones. Our estranged hearts will find their way home once we set them free. They were created with their own compasses already in place. Why are we so slow to trust them?

Elsewhere in this book we will reflect on more inward ways of listening to our hearts and their urgent pleas. Directed meditation, for instance, and guided imagery are most effective and dynamic streams that reach the great underground river of love. There are, in fact, many paths and windows that open out to another land, this other way of being, that is at once both familiar and strange. One such way is called "art-as-meditation." This is a mode of extrovert self-expression that brings art and spirituality together in a creative form. It usually involves dancing, clay-work, painting, music, drama and storytelling. The imagination is brought into play and the healing and uniting begins to happen. It is in the creative imagination that we most closely resemble our creator. That is why, when we have found our center, there is a focusing of our power, an outburst of compassion, a new hunger for justice. Centering is about the release of love.

Rather than in the intelligence, "it may be more realistic," Gregory Baum suggests, "and ultimately more profound to say that faith resides in the imagination." Imagination has to do with the world of wonder. It is because we can imagine that we can trust. It is because we can imagine that we can create. Incarnation was the ultimate expression of the divine imagination. The bodying forth of beauty, the physical shaping of the spirit, the fleshing of inspiration, the final annihilation of dualism—all of these revelations point to the still center of the kingdom within. When Christianity was young, Tertullian preached: "It is on the flesh that salvation is hinged." It is in our bodies that redemption and resurrection happen. That is why we look to meditative participation in the creative arts, to free movement and massage, to discover that hidden vitality that opens up to us ever-new windows of wonder.

If these windows of our perception were kept open, every moment would become an epiphany, a special window of revelation when the focus shifts and a rock becomes a prophecy, a smile signals incarnate forgiveness and a tear is the silent scream of the world's pain. In centering we bring a heightened awareness to all our activities, an attentiveness to every detail, a new way of being present to what is happening. Mundane tasks can then become centering rituals—the cutting open of an orange so that its life-juice may nourish a sickly child; the baking of a cake combining the fruit of the earth with the work of human hands; the cleaving in two of a piece of wood and reading inside it the story of God's presence amongst us for the very first time; the making of the living room fire, an elemental ceremony that links us with the first morning that fire came to the earth. These are all sacred and centering experiences of disclosure that vibrate deeply in the wellsprings of our consciousness, shaking down so many shadows clinging to the walls of our spirit. In such moments do we become intensely aware of the exciting, tremendous lover at our deepest center.

> In the stillness of the night I have walked in your streets, and my spirit has entered your house;
> And your heartbeats were in my heart, and your breath was upon my face, and I knew you all.[8]

SELF-ESTEEM

God's Work of Art

"Hey there, you got 'tude man?" people used to ask me when I arrived out here in northern California to begin my course in creation spirituality. (Not wanting to appear untrendy I would click my fingers, gyrate my creaky hips and venture an incoherent reply which could be taken either way.) With hindsight I imagine I was being questioned about my attitude ('tude) to life in general and to myself in particular. Self-esteem might be another name for it. I wish to examine, in this reflection, the concept of "self-esteem" which is a central theme in this book. It seems to be a combination of micro-attitude—self-image, self-worth, self-identity—with a macro-outlook—one's fundamental option, basic mindset, worldview. Ideally, our self-esteem is not inflexibly fixed, but subject to many influences. It is a compound attitude formed through hereditary and environmental factors, colored strongly by specific, significant experiences of a "religious" and "relational" nature, particularly in childhood. Because self-esteem is born of the spirit and nourished by it, it has a spiritual dimension. I like to link self-esteem with a spirituality of the heart.

People with good self-esteem have confidence in their ability to impress others favorably and to meet the challenges of each day with success. They can enjoy their own company, know themselves to be resourceful and resilient, anticipate change and clearly believe in themselves. There is a positive option for growth of all kinds, a faith in something greater than the individual, an inner source of strength that has many names. People with self-esteem tend to follow their hearts, to trust a lot and to forgive themselves and others. They are also deeply convinced of the impact of habits of the mind on our sense of self.

> What we *think* we are evolves into what in fact we become. Thus our minds as infants are structured both from within ourselves and from without. To understand how deeply our belief system affects our life and how it develops, it may be helpful to examine three key questions that we answer in early childhood. These involve our sense of power, our sense of competence and our sense of worthwhileness.[9]

Marsha Sinetar emphasizes the experiences of childhood in the formation of these three qualities. Even after traumatic beginnings, the resilience of some children may see them through. But in almost all instances where the above three characteristics of self-esteem are weak or missing, the damage was done in the early years.

> . . . it is from the business of childhood that our adult working life takes shape. This includes our ability to identify what it is we want to do in life, the happiness we allow ourselves to reach for, the way we solve or avoid problems, our willingness to stand apart from the crowd, our ability to take responsibility for our decisions, and our ability to be responsible for the goals we set.[10]

People with good self-esteem have the golden thread that connects their images, their motivation, their goals and their self-evaluation. With this connectedness the power flows—and not just in a closed circuit within. Self-esteem thrives on participating in the network of relationships that are life-supporting, stretching from self to others to environment in a self-enriching but mutually renewing cycle. For lasting and secure self-esteem it is important that we widen the scope and deepen the knowledge of our self-understanding. I am referring here to the way we see ourselves in the human community context and against the wider context of the universe itself. We are swiftly becoming more aware of the interconnectedness and interdependence of all creation. This understanding of ourselves as part of a whole, as a vital link in the network of living things, as a brother and sister to every other human being on the planet and to all non-two-legged creatures and growing things as well—all this wisdom serves only to enhance our self-esteem because of the amazing nature of our identity. To realize that we are made from the energy of the first Big Bang twenty billion years ago, that we are literally constituted of the stuff of the stars, that we humans are the consciousness of the cosmos, that all our ancestors are champions because we exist at all—to realize, even in an elementary fashion just a little of this mystery is to develop a profound sense of self-acceptance, self-worth, self-determination and, above all, self-identity. That is why an understanding of our origins and evolution is so important to our self-knowledge.

As well as having at least an introductory grasp of what is going on in the world of cosmology today for acquiring a healthy and balanced sense of self-identity, some acquaintance with the rediscovered spirituality of the mystics seems highly desirable. Against a rather pessimistic view of the beginning of the world as we know it, creation spirituality and incarnational theology paint a compelling and exciting picture of our universe as the love-child of a God who is crazy about everything that he has made. Not alone is the cosmos carefully crafted by a divine artist of awesome beauty, but we humans are the daughters and sons of that same Father and Mother, exquisitely brought to birth in their sacred image, and empowered by the spirit of their infinite love. How could those of us who believe in such an unbelievable state of affairs ever suffer from low self-esteem? In a world where fortunes change with alarming frequency, where the high and mighty are regularly scattered forever like leaves in a storm, how secure is my self-esteem without the cosmic and divine connection that gives me my eternal birthright? As long as I settle for ephemeral "off-the-rack" relationships and disconnected, addictive affairs with shallow allurements rather than letting go into the intimate fusion with my heart's desire, how can I ever assume the undreamt-of stature for which I was so elegantly designed before time began?

The worlds of the artist, the physicist and the mystic hold the windows of wonder about which this book is written. It is offered as a place of connection for establishing the *reasons* that lead to high self-esteem before discussing its characteristics and strategies for its nurture. What is breathtaking about these infancy narratives—those of the cosmos, those of the Christ and those of each child—is the sweeping power of their vision of exquisite beauty and love. The scientist and the theologian unite in wonder at the revelations and possibilities that continue to evoke astonishment as Lady Mystery graciously unfolds her secrets.

> It is the whole of nature—from the protons to a Schubert sonata—which is glorified by the indwelling of God. It is the whole of creation—not just humanity—which marches toward the Parousia. Perhaps Dante saw it all over 600 years ago in his final vision of Paradise when all that which is scattered throughout the universe is fused together in a simple ineffable light, *legato con amore in un volume*— bound by love in one volume.[11]

We catch glimpses of the splendor of this wholeness at odd moments during our lives. We all carry echoes of this wonder in our hearts. Where does the original vision come from? And what happens to this vaguely remembered blueprint of our proud destiny? How is it recovered? Does it ever come true? And when it does, will it be for each of us at different times, or for the human race as a whole, or is every step forward linked with the future of the universe itself?

These are exciting and profound questions. Maybe some-one has the answers. This book offers one possible setting against which such questions might be asked. "Living the ques-tions raw" seems a better option just now rather than hoping for definitive solutions. I end this reflection with some practical suggestions about enhancing personal self-esteem at the present moment with a final comment about the hope of a wider cosmic renaissance in the decades to come.

Although the pursuit of self-esteem requires a self-aware-ness and self-acceptance that comes from silence and discipline, it is still one of the most exciting journeys of all. It demands commitment and patience, trust and letting go, and it costs "not less than everything" as T.S. Eliot puts it with reference to attaining that "condition of simplicity" which is the "work of the saints." It is in our handling of the difficulties—the surprise conflicts, the frequent disappointments, the moments of doubt —that some kind of evaluation can be made. Progress will usually be slow, but once we sense that we are going with the current, that we are tapped into, and supported by, the divine energy that drives all creation to its goal, we are not depressed anymore by failure and severe challenges. There is an awesome power to be harnessed when such synergism is focused in the interests of self-esteem.

There is an intrinsic and fertile coming together of head,

heart and body especially when such connecting is receptive to the waves of wisdom that flow throughout the universe. We respond in our totality to our fully internalized goals, dreams and allurements. Self-esteem is built with the fabric of thoughts, words, actions and images. We self-talk our esteem to an appropriate level by affirmations and meditation. A certain kind of "taking hold" of our lives is necessary for healthy self-esteem. We decide to make life happier for others. We believe that we build self-esteem not by searching for more of anything but by letting go of what we have. I am being created when I help you to create. In one sense we have the ever-present paradox playing in our hearts again: it is in self-forgetfulness that we achieve self-esteem. We then enjoy the love of others. "True self-esteem can be found only in the reflected appraisal of those whom we have loved," wrote Viktor Frankl. Like dreams and mirrors, true love cannot lie.

Alone, it is difficult to press ahead. We need certain people around us to inspire us in many ways to live up to our capacities, to persevere against all the odds, to take a great number of risks each day. Without some kind of role models we struggle unnecessarily. And without emotional support we must surely give up. It is not always obvious that there are those who are ready, willing and able to offer support, comfort, challenge, understanding and love, people who recognize our uniqueness in different ways and encourage us to belong. These exceptional lovers are to be openly cherished.

But no emotional support group can make our decisions. To allow this would be to contribute to our condition of powerlessness. My personal power is reclaimed when I assert my choices as my own, when I clearly make known my needs and opinions, and when I realize that I am free to change my negative thought patterns and capable of actually doing so. Ultimately I, and I alone, am responsible for my worldview. In *Getting Unstuck*, Dr. Sidney Simon describes the potential of negative self-fulfilling prophecies for maintaining zero self-esteem. "Write a letter to the year ahead," he advises, by way of beating the destructive habit:

> Think of next year as a close friend and in your letter tell that friend about the success you anticipate, the risks you hope to take, the tasks you want to accomplish, and all your other goals.[12]

Another central principle is to set your own self-esteem standards. What must be constantly combatted is the false list of criteria set by the popes of consumerism and subliminally beamed into us every day. In light of the cults of beauty, youth, fashion, fitness and possessions, it is vital to keep resetting our thermostats of value and worth, reforming and repairing the constantly assaulted spiritual dimension of our assessments. We need confidence in what our hearts tell us—the dream, the instinct, the internal monitor—resisting external comparisons and pressures, focused as they are on human weakness rather than on human strength.

There is a spreading pattern of loving throughout the land which affects the universal as well as the individual. It is to the same dawn of hope and completion that the eyes of the personal heart and the pain-wracked body of the universe wake. There is an ever-widening conspiracy of lovers of mother earth whose dreams are vibrant with truth and power, and whose hearts reflect the justice and peace that will surely be established soon. The center of this healing movement is the network of artists, or rather the networking of the artistry in everyone—in those who express their creativity in the ecstasy of their passion for whatever allures them, from the telling of a story to the diving in a pool. Never before was there a time when ecclesiastical institutions, secular establishments and national governments expressed their concern and committed their support in the interests of ecology, environmental issues and conservation.[13] And never before were individuals as enthusiastic about exploring their creativity, following their hearts, committing themselves to their bliss, and in so doing, bringing the original vision, the primal dream, another step along the way.

UNCONDITIONAL LOVE

Testing the Limits

We are not strangers to the destructive forces within us. We are well aware of their fatal attraction. It is also true, and for the reasons outlined above, that in its essential nature love too is awesome in its power. Human love tends toward totality—the totality of the freedom of the beloved. In its essence it is ordered toward non-possessiveness and the welfare of the person, community or cause that is loved. Because all life is seen as intrinsically valuable beyond description, one dies repeatedly in trying to love unconditionally. We have the perfect model for such a fundamental option. In Christ's human love, with his many small deaths before his final letting go into the love that he trusted, we have an eternal paradigm for unconditional love. From the loneliness and separation in Christ's life and death we can gather that the seeds of death are sown into all life and love. There is a sharp edge to the reality of unconditional love. It is filled with separation, loneliness and hints of death.

We are here at the heart of mystery. It would appear that for unconditional love to be redemptive, to continue burning brightly and surely, it must be daily fueled by a thousand sacrificial deaths. While we have our litanies of great martyrs and hallowed lists of saints—men and women whose courage and endurance in testifying to a limitless kind of loving inspire us again and again to look within at our own potential—yet, in hidden crucibles of pain all over the world, there are silent sacrifices lived every night and every day, where deep in the human heart there happen victories of love that are celebrated forever in heaven.

> Life is filled with impossible loves, with people who have had to reach across chasms of separation to support and sustain each other. Some of the deepest and most responsible love that I have seen in this life has been mysteriously present outside of marriage. . . . I have seen it in people kept apart by illness or other obligations of caring for sick relatives—lovers who have had to face unexpected sacrifices for the sake of others. And I have seen, in the complexities of real life, men and women reach across the boundaries of marriage itself to give support and strength to others without breaking the vows of either marriage. I have seen love like this, a love seldom written or spoken about, but a love whose source is in the Spirit, and it is a love that gives life as it gives everything and can take nothing in return.[14]

Not many have had the experience of being loved unconditionally. In childhood particularly, where growing is synonymous with adapting, imitating and adjusting, the love of our parents seems dependent on our capacity to conform to their expectations of our development. As children we are ready to change ourselves in all kinds of ways to merit and hold parental love. And here somewhere is the beginning of a long and tragic story, because we learn to suppress our anger, our sexuality and our innate sense of justice in the desperate effort to deserve the most important love in our young lives. We are loved, it seems to us as children, conditionally. We, in our turn, continue to love conditionally. Conditional on change: "I will love you if . . ." "I will love you more when . . ." We grow up in a world of reward and punishment, of comparisons and competition, of judging and criticizing, of merited love.

Here lies the reason for the strange difficulty many people have in accepting the concept, and certainly the reality, of unconditional love. On two occasions recently when I was reflecting aloud on the universality of divine unconditional forgiveness, I was forcefully taken to task for spreading false rumors. Such speculation was dangerous. It sinned against the positive persuasion of fear, the justice of God and revealed truth. More often than not the aggression comes from adults who were never hugged by their parents, who never experienced much in the way of freely bestowed forgiveness and who, as children, were never asked to forgive their often manipulative parents.

It is almost impossible to experience a person without evaluating that person, or to evaluate without judging, or to judge without condemning. A brief, honest look into our own hearts will convince us of that state of affairs. There is much projection going on here. We still carry around with us the parental tape of fault-finding and critical evaluation of our behavior. When we play it, and we always do, we deal with this crippling voice of blame, by blaming in return. It becomes a destructive habit of mind, making growth impossible. We are the ones who suffer. Our confidence is killed. Everything we send out comes back to us.

The experience of being loved unconditionally is a rare gift. It works wonders for our self-image, our confidence and our self-esteem. We know we can only claim it for our own by blessing others with the same grace: to love without judging; to forgive without desiring improvement; to pledge friendship forever with no strings attached; to regard each encountered person as either extending love generously or as fearful and silently pleading for acceptance with no conditions. We find it hard to believe that this is the only way for our own spirit to become truly rich and passionate. We only keep what we give away. It was pointed out during the famous banquet in "Babette's Feast" that our beauty in heaven will be created by what we have let go of here.

Like an early spring day entices the small flowers to wake up and the new life to venture forth so too our fundamental option for unconditional love is full of gentle power.

> . . . *your slightest look easily will unclose me*
> *though I have closed myself as fingers,*
> *you open always petal by petal myself as Spring opens*
> *(touching skillfully, mysteriously) her first rose . . .*[15]

In the current of unconditional love we become creative and powerful. These are the waters of inspiration and healing. The more we abandon ourselves to them, the more grace-filled we become. They will support us, enrapture us and bring us to an exhilaration we never knew before. We are flowing with and floating in the underground tide of love. "If you trust the river of life," Krishnamurti was fond of saying, "the river of life has an astonishing way of taking care of you." Loving unconditionally is to our hearts what air, food and exercise are to our bodies and minds. The only goal that is recognized as worthwhile by the spirit within is that of achieving a condition of free-flowing forgiveness always and for everything. A lived trust in love and in our capacity to become that same divine love is the sun and soil of our spiritual growth. This is the climate for which we were created. This is the only becoming that is worthy of our life's commitment. Everything else is flawed, or misleading, or severely destructive of that sacred but fragile desire to be perfect as God is perfect, to continue saving the world by dying for it.

While our aim is to be continually testing the limits of the infinite sea of our hearts it is often in small decisions and spontaneous moments that progress is made or lost. Our innate allurement is toward unconditional trust in unconditional love so that by virtue of the incarnation we become that love, actualizing and realizing what we already are. This vision is incarnated slowly. Even in seemingly insignificant daily reactions and decisions there will often be a wild kind of extravagance, a refusal to calculate our generosity, to place conditions on our loving. What one strives for is a condition of openness that transcends our closedness, an interiorized option for trusting and letting go. There are those who acquire a second-nature predisposition, continually nourished by a regular communion with beauty, for unerring accuracy in cutting through the fog of hidden prejudice, false self-justification, insecurity and fear. After a while, doing the loving thing comes naturally.

Our deepest longing is for unconditional love. Merited or "deserved" love has a serious uncertainty about it. That is why unconditional love is more than a deep emotion, a humanitarian feeling. Unconditional loving is based on a commitment. We *decide*. It is not dependent on changing conditions. The marriage vows, for instance, express in accurate words this vision of the potential of human nature. Such love is transforming. There is no greater power. The beloved becomes confident of his worth and is set free to be himself more and more completely. Unconditional love graces the other person with the gift of herself. When I am loved unconditionally I can see myself as valuable in the eyes of the lover; in the stillness of such a changeless love my own beauty is mirrored so that I can truly love myself for the first time in my life. And then I am free to empower the world with my own precious love. This is when the network of salvation is extended, when the conspiracy of redeemers surfaces in a new location, when the epidemic of a crazy kind of loving breaks out all over the place. Christians speak about the building of the kingdom.

There is a deep resistance to the possibility of unconditional love, in both the giving and receiving. There are false fears, of losing one's identity, one's freedom. That is to confuse love with fusion. "Love consists in this," wrote Rainer Maria Rilke, "that two solitudes protect and touch and greet each other." True love offers roots (for a sense of belonging) and wings (for a sense of independence and freedom). There is a space between that must remain empty. It is across this space that the en-couragement happens, the empowering of the other to believe in the self, the challenging toward transcendence, the call to explore the rich delights of the promised land of one's own heart, the reminding of each one's responsibility to save, heal and redeem the other.

The most explosive truth that I am sure of seems so ordinary. It is that love is all. Most of us will have learned this along the way, with our heads. But there are rare moments of disclosure when our hearts light up and the world is changed forever.

And, as we stumbled along for miles, slipping on icy spots, supporting each other time and again, dragging one another up and onward, nothing was said, but we both knew; each of us was thinking of his wife. Occasionally I looked at the sky, where the stars were fading and the pink light of the morning was beginning to spread behind a dark bank of clouds. But my mind clung to my wife's image, imagining it with an uncanny acuteness. I heard her answering me, saw her smile, her frank and encouraging look.

A thought transfixed me: for the first time in my life I saw the truth as it is set into song by so many poets, proclaimed as the final wisdom by so many thinkers. The truth—that love is the ultimate and the highest goal to which humans can aspire. Then I grasped the meaning of the greatest secret that human poetry and human thought and belief have to impart: the salvation of humanity is through love and in love.[16]

SUMMARY

Preparing for High Self-Esteem

I have used selected themes from this summary (and from the other three summaries at the end of each "Window" section), in our most recent *Windows of Wonder* workshop days.

1. The Dream

In the beginning was the dream and the dream was with God and the dream was God. We are part of God's dream. God dreams in us. Can you remember your childhood dreams? Trailing clouds of glory, you were the center of the world. You would spread love and joy everywhere; you would change the face of the earth. Your life would be as happy as the bright day was long. Are you living your dream now or did someone steal it? Or did it die? Daniel Levinson said that we weep at the distance between what we now are and what we once dreamed of becoming. We will recover this dream: it is our first Window of Wonder.

2. Hidden Beauty

Beginning the journey inward; the search for the hidden beauty, the half-remembered dream, the quiet place of wonder.

Deep within is the real you: "May your hidden self grow strong" is the wish of St. Paul. We try to honor our own mystery. We come from God, full of brightness and beauty. It is all still there because God is at our center wanting to love us into deep joy and peace. All of this is an old and beautiful story of loveliness, often forgotten in our fear and doubt. God's love is at the heart of all things, but especially at the center of your own.

3. Images and Glimpses

The mystics saw God's great love as an underground river, deep and powerful. We wheel around like leaves in a puddle, like struggling streams until we find our way into the strong, inviting flow of the current of love. Or God's love can be imaged as the bright ray of light that gives meaning to the dark negative that we are without him, as the projector explodes this small, murky slide into brilliant color. God's intimate love is the flow and the color in all creation but especially in us, made as we are in his own very image. So there are glimpses of his beauty all around us. But our hearts are clouded and we don't always see very clearly. This is the work of the mystic in all of us—to recapture the vision again, to dream the dream again and make it come true.

4. The Original Vision

The vision we search for, the sun we seek, the kingdom of God we wish to inhabit is safe and well within us—but we have wandered far from that land of beauty. We lived in it as children, our faces alive with wonder, our eyes shining with praise. We were small mystics then, full of play, open to the miracle of each new day, trusting our wondering hearts very, very close to God:

> ... *it was all*
> *Shining; it was Adam and maiden.*
> *So it must have been after the birth of*
> *the simple light*
> *in the first spinning place* ...[17]

5. Where Is My Heart?

Does my heart remember that vision? Somewhere along
our journey through the decades did we lose sight of something
precious? In the pursuit of another attraction did we forget the
allurement of our heart? Why, in spite of the comforts and
lifestyles we have achieved, are we restless for another way of
being, another place where our spirits are nourished, another
land where our souls are more free? Our passion, you see, is for
the things of the spirit, but I exchange that passion for desires
that do not fulfill. We are made, as St. Paul reminds us, to be
"completely filled with the very nature of God," but instead
there is a famine of the heart. Today is the time to begin listening to our deeper selves; "to thine own self be true."

6. God's Work of Art

How could we not have self-esteem when we reflect on our
dignity and glory? "You are God's work of art" (St. Paul). "We
are daughters and sons of the Tremendous Lover" (Francis
Thompson). "When we are truly human it is God's glory"
(Irenaeus). Is my "hidden self" growing stronger? Do I always
remember that it is in God's love that I live and move and have
my being? How unique and precious that makes me, how truly
wonder-ful. My self-value, self-worth and self-esteem are daily
growing because I am created with infinite care by the God of
the universe and loved into life each day by his extravagant and
delighted devotion to my well-being. There are, therefore, some

magic mornings when my breathless heart is weak with thanksgiving.

7. God's Image

We are designed and fashioned with infinite care right from the beginning by our loving creator. It is God's delight to be at our deepest center, always perfecting his image in us if we but allow him. He is the indwelling grace, forever trying to shine through. St. Paul speaks of us as God's work of art, to be completely filled with the very nature of God. St. Bernard speaks of God as our inner glory which must shine out. Irenaeus reminds us that our fullest humanity is God's glory.

Meister Eckhart tells us that just as the pear seed becomes a pear tree and the hazel seed a hazel tree, so too God's seed in us blossoms in godliness, when God becomes all in all. Karl Rahner's theology is about God's desire in love to create humanity and then to become it. The Jesuit poet Gerard Manley Hopkins writes of a world that is "charged with the grandeur of God" because the Holy Ghost broods over the world "with warm breast and with ah! bright wings."

8. Epiphanies

Because of Christ's life—the incarnation of God's love on earth—all creation is an epiphany and revelation of God. The heavens and earth show forth his glory; he is the God of all creation; "all life, all holiness comes from you." We are "other Christs." St. Teresa of Avila wrote: "Christ has no body now on earth but yours; no hands but yours; no feet but yours; yours are the eyes through which is to look out Christ's compassion to the world; yours are the feet through which he is to go about doing good; yours are the hands through which he is to bless people now."

The God of Jesus is a God of surprises, forever turning up in the most unexpected places. This is another lesson that we are slow to learn from the incarnation. There is a story about God's wish to play hide-and-seek with human beings. He asked for advice. None of the suggestions were proving helpful—e.g. behind the highest mountain peak, at the bottom of the deepest ocean, on the moon . . . Human beings had been everywhere. It was then that his advisor exclaimed, "I know! Hide in the human heart; they will never think of looking for you there!"

9. The Cosmic Story

The amazing story of our evolution is a basis for self-esteem. It is God's compassion that created and sustains all life. Humanity comes at the end of a long line of exciting development. There are many new insights into the love story that began with creation and reached a high point in incarnation. Never before was the mystery of our existence, both as a universe and as human beings, revealed to be so full of wonder.[18]

St. Bonaventure points out that "in creation we see the footprints of God." Accounts of the shining through, the sense of unity, the harmonious peace, epiphanies of the holy, are readily available from research centers, from the stories of our friends and from within our own hearts. My friend Kathleen wrote to me about the following "moment" which took place one evening in a Rathmore field, many years ago, in County Kerry—a place that has its own special kind of magic:

> We walked together in the field. I can never forget the spot where it happened. I was barefoot on the green grass. My Dad was beside me. It seemed like he was totally present to me and to all of nature. I remember feeling that his love, just then, was unconditional. And then something happened. It seemed like I connected with the trees, the wild

flowers, the stones, the birds, the whole universe, my Dad and my own heart. A moment stood still in time. It was so powerful. That moment has stayed with me ever since. I became a child of nature. I connected with everything in the cosmos.

Because of that moment I was never the same again. I could immediately see all that was phony. I could detect what was natural and what was real. I rejected the unreal and the artificial almost with a sixth sense. Nobody could ever destroy me after that moment because from then on, I somehow understood everything . . .

In a relaxed state, and with appropriate music, it is possible for most of us to return to a rich but perhaps forgotten time when we looked, just for a moment, through a window of bright wonder.

10. *Guided Imagery for a "Moment of Wonder" Meditation*

Move into a comfortable position, relaxed and easy. Become aware of your breathing, deep and unforced. Don't try to change it. Let the music flow around you.

Become aware of your heartbeat, pulsing life throughout your veins. Feel the warm glow of energy reaching to all parts of your body. Follow the sensation coming from your stomach to your chest, and along your arms and legs, reaching your face and relaxing it, softening it here and there.

Your love is springing from a well deep inside you, and flowing out from you, up to and through your skin, from your eyes and fingertips.

Now gently begin to move toward a very special moment in your life—in childhood or more recently. It may have been a wondrous scene in nature, a sunrise, a sunset . . . maybe a warm summer's day with a perfect breeze . . . the sound and sight of waves beating toward the shore . . . the fresh air of high mountains, beautiful against the sky . . .

Revisit this special moment of wonder and joy in your imagination. Do not hold back on it. What are the tastes, sights, scents and sounds? Notice the time of day or night. What were you wearing? Who were you with? Was anything said? Relive the emotions. Experience those feelings again without hurry or effort.

Stay there for a little while. It is a moment when God is loving you in a very special way.

Second Window

The Wonder of Darkness

GRIEF

Love's Dark Companion

"If we choose to love we must have the courage to grieve." Not many lovers, however, work it out beforehand just like that. If they did, I wonder how many would travel those paths of high drama, of passion and power, of pathos and tragedy, of terrible despair, and sometimes, indeed, of final destruction. But the heart will not be told. It has, according to Pascal, "reasons that Reason knows not of." I sometimes think that no power on earth can control the precipitous surging of a heart in full cry, pursuing relentlessly the beauty and ecstasy that unforgivingly allures it. My opinion is based on the great stories and myths of the world as well as on what I occasionally observe going on in my own heart when it thinks I'm not looking.

If you dare to love, be prepared to grieve. To live is to know that this is true. Each heart has its own secret drama, its own sacred story. And each heart is changed in different ways by the experience of love and grief. At one end there are those hearts that become ever more open and vulnerable to the impact of love and loss, to the power and pain of the world. These mystical spirits have truly incarnated the compassion of God. At the other extreme there are those frightened souls that have not mourned their loss and whose love-wounds remain raw. They withdraw from pain. To achieve this, they know full well, they must avoid love too. It is not by chance that Simon and Garfunkel's song remains a classic:

> *I have no need for friendship; friendship causes pain.*
> *I am a rock, I am an island.*
> *If I never loved I never would have cried.*
> *A rock can feel no pain; an island never cries.*

Whatever way one looks at it, grieving is built into the heart of life. Because the growing kind of love always means having to let go. And letting go is never easy. Deepening one's love entails deepening one's loss; for the baby bird to fly it must let go of its last hold on security; to love you fully I must fully let you go. That is why loving and mourning are never far apart. In fact, I suspect, they are not different at all. Perhaps we separate them because we are creatures in space and time, our spirit limited within our finite condition. The rich texture of divine compassion is woven, the poets say, from the twin threads of love and grief, forming a way of being, a design of beauty, an exquisite pattern of relating, the occasional glimpse of which makes our hearts ache as the heart of the lonely exile aches for its native land.

We may have stumbled here to a window on this mysterious dance of love and grief. All love has to do with intimacy, completion, and oneness, all grief with separation. In a world of time and of space, of growing and of changing, love and grief will be twin-travelers and will be found everywhere. The first cry of a baby is usually one of separation-anxiety as it grieves for the womb; the last cry of the Son of God on the cross was one of separation-anxiety as he grieved for his Father. Is it any wonder that our lives, at their deepest center, are always in a state of mourning—and why is this a good thing?

Grieving is good because it is the natural child of love and longs only to heal us. Jesus wept and his Father sheds many a tear these days, and their mourning is redemptive. Mourning, if you think about it, has intense power. It has all the power of love and more. There is a fine edge to it that cuts through normally accepted limitations. Some of the finest breakthroughs in human history were achieved at the point of the moment of grief. Creation spirituality is insistent on the potential for creativity in the darkness and silence of loss. One can almost hear the ache in the great music of the composer who wrote from his despair or in the creations of the painter whose brush-strokes are made by her mourning heart. Something of God is burning inside the soul that is whirl-swept in the passionate currents of love and grief. This explosive power often erupts from disbelieving shock, cold anger, deep despair, relentless guilt or grey loneliness. The mystics describe such moments as the *via negativa*—the dark womb from which birthing happens, the sense of loss that precedes a new fullness, the way of healing and inspiration, the *via creativa* of creation spirituality.

In his book *Grief and Growth*, R. Scott Sullender writes about the new vision that grows from the time of grieving. He sees grief as a reordering or restructuring of chaos. Creativity is about putting raw experience together in a new way. Chaos is the result of the loss of structure brought about by the occasion of grief. There is a faint call toward restructuring. The imagination is brought in to play and creativity is underway. According to Sullender, loss events have a way of initiating periods of rapid growth—or self-destructive regret and bitterness. This is why it is so important to know how to mourn in a healthy way, to become familiar with our grief. Who will empower us into creativity through a transcendence of our sorrow? There is a powerful ceremony for the death of a friend; where is the ritual for the death of a friendship? The deepest symbolism abounds on the occasion of the public commitment of a couple at the beginning of their marriage. Where are the rites to mark its ending?

We need sacramentals—little ceremonies—to facilitate expressions of grief on the occasion of all kinds of losses: every separation anticipates the final one and recalls the first one—this is why traveling, airports, even holidays can be such ambiguous experiences touching intimate spiritual chords of our souls. The ritual will provide the space for connecting and expressing what is going on in us—it will place things in perspective in a community context, offering understanding and hope. To change one's residence, to lose a limb, to become unemployed, to reach mid-life, to become dependent, to say the last goodbye, to lose vitality—most of us are familiar with one or other of these deeply emotional and spiritual events, and how we handle them is of crucial significance to the quality of our lives. "Dealing with mortality means that a person must engage in mourning for the dying self of youth, so that the self can be made more whole." Daniel Levinson here underlines the need for a ministry of mourning. It is a neglected goldmine of spiritual power.

It is impossible to even attempt a hierarchy of losses. Any loss can be devastating. What is shrugged off by one as a temporary challenge can drive another to suicide. A separation that one partner transcends after an appropriate period of mourning will keep the other locked into a relentless pit of despair. In my own pastoral experience one of the keenest and most lasting sorrows arises from the death of a child. The advent of each birthday and the turning of the seasons become a perennial calendar of pure pathos. I wish to finish with a few words about mourning the dead.

Isadora Duncan lost both her young children when a taxicab in which they were riding fell into the water. After their death she fled to the home of her Italian friend, the actress Eleonora Duse, to be consoled in her enormous loss. In *My Life* she wrote:

She used to rock me in her arms, consoling my pain, but not only consoling, for she seemed to take my sorrow to her own breast, and I realized that if I had not been able to bear the society of other people, it was because they all played the comedy of trying to cheer me with forgetfulness. Whereas Eleonora said, "Tell me about Patrick and Deirdre," and made me repeat to her all their little sayings and ways, and show their photos, which she kissed and cried over. She never said "Cease to grieve," but she grieved with me, and for the first time since their death I felt I was not alone.

Grieving is life-giving. But it is rarely seen as such. In fact society does not take kindly to public displays of sorrow. And even in private, as Isadora discovered, friends try to comfort the bereaved by distracting them from their sorrow. Everything that facilitates the normal expressions of grief contributes to health and wholeness. There was great power, for instance, in the traditional words, symbols and music of many old-time religious services on the occasion of death and burial. The Roman Catholic funeral rites included dark vestments, a haunting Latin melody, cosmic redeeming words at the graveside, the raw moment of truth when the coffin was lowered into the earth, and the shocking sound of the pebbles against the buried wood. This is one of the few times that a person has the local community's permission to mourn in public. It is of the greatest importance that the mourning begins immediately. Early appropriate expressions of grief are significantly therapeutic in enabling the emotions to catch up with the way things now are, with making the loss "real." The task of grief is to let go into the truth, to adjust the psyche to the new reality. The process cannot be forced, because emotions have their own timing; the danger lies in the fact that people easily "get stuck" in one or other of the "stages."

Denied, suppressed or sidetracked sorrow will fester and destroy. This is especially true in the event of intense bereavement. The sense of loss is acute; the spirit is devastated; the mind is immobilized; the heart is broken. The journey to acceptance and eventual growth and transcendence of the pain will, ideally, begin immediately. This journey will involve accusations and blaming, denying and feeling guilty, depression and tiredness. These emotions will ebb and flow like waves over the sand. At unexpected moments they will return to open the healing wound, but less frequently and with less intensity. And the grief process can be trusted. It is on the side of the living.

The following suggestions may help those who are recently bereaved.

Take time for, and trust, nature's slow, sure, uneven process of healing. It will help you at first to recognize and realize the loss.

Give yourself massive doses of restful relaxation and routine work. (Most bereaved people tend to distract themselves by overwork.)

Believe that your overwhelming despair will become less intense.

Stay vulnerable, share your suffering, try to accept support.

Talk about the person who has died; share stories with friends.

Use mementos to facilitate your mourning. These could be part of any rituals you may devise with friends during the most difficult months.

Avoid rebound relationships, important decisions and anything addictive.

Write daily to record your feelings; do not suppress your tears when alone or with friends.

Prepare for change, new interests, new friends, more time alone.

Recognize that forgiveness (of ourselves and others) is a vital part of the healing process.

Know that holidays, anniversaries, special days will bring up the painful feelings you thought you had worked through.

Realize that any new death-related crises will restimulate emotions arising from past losses.

There is one last ray of light that dispels some of the heavier clouds of grief and despair that so often seem so reluctant to move. I have found it strangely comforting to remember that no moment of my sorrow is wasted. This thought brings me a harvest-feeling of hope for tomorrow. In her book *Sharing the Darkness*, Sheila Cassidy expresses this most movingly:

> I believe
> no pain is lost.
> The blood
> shed in Salvador
> will irrigate the heart
> of some financier
> a million miles away.
> The terror,
> pain,
> despair,
> swamped
> by lava, flood or earthquake
> will be caught up
> like mist and fall again,
> a gentle rain
> on arid hearts
> or souls despairing
> in the back streets
> of Brooklyn.[1]

LETTING GO

The Perennial Paradox

Deep in most of us there lies a fascination for liberation from the forces that press and stifle our spirit, because there is a tension that exists in our hearts between possessiveness and letting go, between clinging and setting free, between settling and exploring. This is a persistent condition of our lives and on the balance hangs our growth and peace. There are allurements that are blinding, attractions that are fatal. There are compulsions to stay young looking, to be admired, to be powerful. Even the pursuit of virtue can be ambiguous. Gandhi felt compelled to let go of his desire for results, of his hopes of success so as to attain to his *atman* and thus remain true to his essential vision. The grace of letting go needs to be at the heart of all our passions, even of the urgent commitment to justice, to peace and to freedom. The story is told about the woman who adroitly cornered Metropolitan Anthony Bloom one morning after service and gleefully told him the news about her spiritual growth. "I have acquired almost all the virtues," she gushed, "and have only two vices to be vanquished." "For God's sake," the archbishop replied, "hang on to those two vices."

All letting go is basically the letting go of being a victim of our emotions, especially of our fear. We will always feel the anger, jealousy, inferiority, but letting go is about not *indulging* in them or being crippled or stifled by them. We take the responsibility for our mental and emotional condition. We will always have moments of depression or frustration, but these emotions will not control our spiritual development. We can do little about our initial reactions to situations but a great deal about what happens after that. It seems that there are two fundamental forces within us—the law of fear which leads to distrust, envy, hoarding and jealousy, and the law of love whose essence it is to let go, to give away, to act positively by trusting, creating, healing, emptying and surprising others with extravagance. A spirituality of the heart reminds us of a strange truth—that all we give away is given to ourselves, that giving of myself increases the love that I am, that "you can only take with you when you die what you let go of when you were alive."

The second of the four paths (or windows) of the mystical tradition of creation spirituality is called the *via negativa*. It is the way of darkness, of silence, of emptiness, and is generally about letting go of security. This surrender can be experienced in terms of small sacrifices or great pain. Either way, darkness and emptiness are apt descriptions of the process. There is loss of direction, a fear of confusion, a temptation to panic. The mystics emphasize the stature of waiting. To let go with grace is to challenge one of our deepest instincts for self-preservation. It is not easy to live with the consequent ambiguity. We crave for certainty. We hope for instant wisdom. We have developed our capacity to know but are very uncomfortable with not knowing, with seeming contradictions, with conflicting principles. It is sometimes too soon to tell. There is a time to withdraw, to wait, to stay with the pain of uncertainty, to balance on the verge, unsure of the safe side to come down on. Gregory Baum has written about the experience of being "marginalized from institutions." It is a precarious time when authority is reclaimed from the external establishments and relocated within. There is a raw and lonely edge to letting go at the center. Becoming "unprogrammed" or "de-conditioned" is a painful exercise. Our "shoulds" put up a gallant fight. There is much panic and resistance from within at the prospect of becoming free. That is why the waiting time is so difficult. There is nothing to *do*. Nobody told us how to let things happen to us.

> *What must I do for Enlightenment?*
>   *Nothing.*
> *Why not?*
>   *Because Enlightenment does not come from doing;*
>   *it happens.*
> *Then can it never be attained?*
>   *Oh yes it can.*
> *How?*
>   *Through nondoing.*
> *And what does one do to attain nondoing?*
>   *What does one do to go to sleep or to wake up?*[2]

A pervading inner anxiety compels us to manipulate the future so that we can avoid the pains of the past and ensure our happiness. For our apprehensive spirits, to wait without planning and scheming is the hardest thing. "It is not unreasonable," Monica Furlong writes, "to try to avoid pain, but manipulation (the success or failure of which sets up acute tension within us) becomes a god in itself, demanding all our attention, cutting us off not only from a degree of suffering and discomfort, but also from unpredictable and spontaneous forms of happiness."[3] Without trusting the empty spaces and the silences there can be no growing. C.G. Jung draws on the insights of creation spirituality to enrich his psychological perspectives on human liberation and spiritual development. He writes:

> The art of letting things happen, action through non-action, letting go of oneself, as taught by Meister Eckhart,

became for me the key opening the door to the way. We must be able to let things happen in the psyche. For us, this actually is an art of which few people know anything. Consciousness is forever interfering, helping, correcting, and negating, and never leaving the simple growth of the psychic processes in peace.[4]

Letting go is a kind of dying. This is a well-worn phrase but it comes with a sharp newness every time we live it through. It is difficult to experience and difficult to image. Letting go is like dying into freedom, like sinking beneath the waves only to find a new security and level of growth. There is usually a clearly identifiable moment of loneliness, doubt and risk—the emptiness, darkness and silence of the *via negativa*—before the point of realization happens. As creation spirituality clarifies, this is where creative energies are experienced. When the waiting is endured without recourse to distractions, when the emptiness is sustained without reaching for fillers, when the temptation for resolution is resisted, then transformation takes place. In the darkness of that womb of waiting there is a purification of consciousness going on, a fine-tuning of sensitivity, an often stressful breaking free of familiar parameters and an exhilarating openness to ever new possibilities. This is the perennial paradox—the way we grow by subtraction, the birth that lies at the heart of death. And even though the letting go never becomes a habit—it is *always* experienced as a kind of dying—it tends toward repetition. Once you have awakened in this way, once your awareness is sharpened through this kind of experience, once you have caught your first glimpse of a whole new alluring vista, then it is virtually impossible to carry on as though these moments had never happened. Our spirit, in spite of a mysterious resistance, is coded for growth and spiritual emergence. This process is food for the soul, it is the grace of the abundant life.

In an amazingly structured economy of spiritual growth, at the fine point of balance between the emptiness of letting go outward and the impulse inward of a creative dynamism, the new life happens. Three momentous breakthroughs come to mind in such birthing of mystery: first the pregnant chaos that preceded creation, then the expectant waiting that issued in incarnation, and finally the painful self-emptying of the divine man in time that was a condition of our salvation. In these three faces of mystery, so the saints and scholars tell us, it was absolutely imperative that there be split-second timing for these unique breakthroughs between spirit and matter to succeed— for the spirit-filled body of the cosmos to come into being, then for love to be fleshed into humanity, and, after that, for resurrection to happen. This paradigmatic pattern, with its dimensions of trusting, letting go, darkness, emptiness, waiting, dying and birth to new life, is discernible in every transformation toward true growth from the tiniest change at the tip of an insect's antenna to the ultimate consecration of all creation. Creation spirituality is about the way we are present to the continually unfolding drama of newness being played out at every moment, in every place and in every detail.

We are allured toward finding our place in the flow of this continuous creating. We are invited to become a part of such a rhythmic birthing. This takes time and timing. After a while it becomes clear that letting go is not so much something we do from time to time but, if we can attain to it, something that becomes a condition of our daily living. In other words, there is never a moment when there is not something to be let go of. A moment's honest reflection will reveal this for most of us. Eventually we reach a way of being where we no more hang on to what delights and enchants us or cling to the beauty that nourishes the spirit than the blossom does to its perfume or the harp to its music—because if everything is to be ours, then nothing must be mine. It is not easy to satisfy in time what is fashioned for infinity. We each identify in our own lives where the patient waiting is appropriate, where the lonely feeling of letting go must be faced.

Some married people must learn to live with many of their desires interrupted by illness, unexpected separations, or the demands of a household of children. Their lives, they learn quickly, are not really their own once they have given themselves over to love. Without patience, they will not have time to let their children grow or to let their own love for each other grow even as it faces the obstacles and difficulties that stand in its way.[5]

There is a peculiar poignancy in the conflict within a mother's heart in the ebb and flow of a loving protection and a loving letting go in the growing of her children. I was talking with Kathleen, a neighbor's child, now a mother in her own right, about these matters. Recently she wrote to me about her feelings: ". . . they teach you how to care for your children as babies and as teenagers; they tell you they must grow up and go away. But they never tell you about letting go; they never tell you it will be so hard, so painful. How can you let them go without you? How can you watch them making mistakes, moving toward danger? They never told you it would pass so fast, that the years would fly. How can you let go in a day what you had for so long? They tell you they were never yours, just on loan for a few short years, but you know they belonged to you. . . . It seems like you are a child again alone; you must build a new life, this time without children." Here in these lines you have the death and here, too, you have the resurrection. There is the death of the vulnerable, possessive heart and the slow empowering of that heart into a new kind of loving. In this respect, as in all of life's wisdom, the seasons of our soul can learn from the seasons of nature. In *Autumn Sonnets*, the North American poet May Sarton writes with touching pathos:

> *If I can let you go as trees let go*
> *their leaves, so casually, one by one;*
> *If I can come to know what they do know,*
> *that fall is the release, the consummation . . .*

. . . then this kind of trust will always ensure the harvest of the spirit—and love will endure.

As I conclude this reflection a warm breeze slips through the window of my upstairs room with a caress of comfort, as though it sensed the struggle going on inside me, because today there are strange whispers of loss and gain echoing around the empty halls of my heart.

LONELINESS

The Shadow of Intimacy

In this reflection I choose the word "loneliness" not to convey the absence of something but the overflowing of something as yet indefinable. This is because in my own experience, and in the stories of my friends, I can discern three aspects of this awareness. By "mystical" loneliness I mean the waves of pain that flood our spirit when, for one reason or another, we glimpse the perfect harmony, unity and love of the absolute essence, the compassionate being we call God. "Cosmic" loneliness is the name I give to the human condition of alienation, experientially felt or not, caused by the relentlessly increasing split between ourselves and our wider body, the universe. The sadness caused by our inability to adequately communicate to others these heart-dreams and the beginnings of our own personal transformation is what I call the "loneliness of change." This uniquely personal loneliness is intensified by the resistance or ridicule with which revelations about one's spiritual growth are often met. What we normally call "loneliness"— that poignant emotion familiar to all of us in song and in story —I will leave for another time.

There is, I believe, a deep-seated loneliness that nothing in this life can assuage. It comes with created humanity. It is a condition of being finite. It is a kind of witness to absolute intimacy. What is peculiar about the loneliness of which I write is the fact that it is most acute when, humanly speaking, it ought not to be there at all. I have noticed that when my heart is most overwhelmed by beauty, when the ecstasy of life is at its keenest, never is loneliness more unbearable than at such moments. Married friends have told me that even in the fine fullness that being deeply in love can bring, even in their unparalleled rapturous love-making, the shadow of an indescribable loneliness is always heavy.

This is a mystical loneliness. It has something to do with being in exile, with having a vague sense of not being at home. Some folk may be quite happy most of the time but carry within them a memory of another land, an anticipation of a future arrival at a familiar shore. Just as most of us have a vague sense of the kind of person we will love, the kind of place or job that will bring us satisfaction and at least temporary fulfillment, so too, at a more profound level, the loneliness we are discussing is like a readiness to recognize a missing dimension of the spirit. The image of birds that are caged from birth comes to mind. They may have lots of room to fly around, to have a family, to eat good food, to work and play, and yet I'm sure they yearn for the wider, higher, spaces they were made to inhabit—spaces that nobody ever told them about. Within us all there is a spark of eternity, a hint of the divine, a small mystic who has designs on the infinite. In some this spark has almost gone out; it is not strong enough to cause any loneliness. But in others it burns so brightly that it carries a permanent ache. This sensation of deep incompletion is, to a greater or lesser extent, endemic to the human heart. It testifies to the eternal nature of our essence and, paradoxically, it grows more intense even as our sensitivity to true love and beauty grows more acute. Maybe that is why Thomas Wolfe is convinced that "loneliness is the central and inevitable fact of human existence."

It is important that we struggle with this emotion and en-

deavor to name it. It is good for our identity, our self-esteem
and our spiritual growth. It makes for unity. We feel more at
home when we can identify the birds that fly over us, the stones
beneath us, the trees around us and the people we encounter
each day. There is revelation too when we recognize the faces of
our heart. We feel we can deal better with our pride and preju-
dices, our depressions and doubts, our lies and lusts and long-
ings, and begin to know them as such. Among the still unde-
fined oceans of passions and yearnings that will not sleep in my
soul, this mystical loneliness daily becomes more familiar. Its
face is friendly but still half-hidden by the shadows of my own
resistance. It is a dark angel of loss yet a bright promise of
tomorrow's harvest. It has to do with a pain-filled "letting go," a
sense of the passingness of things, of the futility of clinging to
what is not enough in the first place. In an extraordinary way,
the tiniest moment of seeming insignificance can suddenly
move and wound the heart at its most vulnerable center—at its
profound desire to at last belong, to be at home with the beauty
that conceived it and gave it birth—moments such as the hesi-
tancy and confusion of an old person negotiating a "simple"
task like crossing an empty street, the expression of love on a
lovely face unaware of the watcher, the glimpse of a new pattern, a sudden, almost subliminal reflection, a chance and fleet-
ing moment of awareness that sends us spinning back to a "forgotten" original vision.

Creation spirituality would bracket the theme of this reflection, so far, as "mystical loneliness." I wish now to move on
to a consideration of what it would refer to as "cosmic loneliness." We are daily becoming more aware of a state of alienation
that has arisen between humanity and the rest of creation. In
recent centuries and especially during the present one, a state of
dis-ease and dis-connectedness has surfaced into the consciousness of an ever-increasing number of those who have a strong
sense of the unity of all things. The universe is seen as a closely

interrelated web of dependencies where the human plays a profoundly significant role. Without the linking there can be no full living. The grounding gives us our basic sense of direction.

> We belong to the ground.
> It is our power.
> And we must stay close to it
> or maybe we will get lost.[6]

The Australian aborigine who wrote those words was a person of innate wisdom. Deeply spiritual too are the insights of native American Indians such as Chief Seattle and Black Elk for whom the earth, the animals, the seasons, the elements of nature and human beings were all part of one body of great beauty, fragility and delicate interdependence.

> The old Lakota was wise. He knew that man's heart away from nature becomes hard. He knew that lack of respect for growing, living things soon led to lack of respect for humans too. So he kept his youth close to its softening influence. So close did some of the Lakotas come to their feathered and furred friends that in true brotherhood they spoke a common tongue.[7]

Uvavnuk, an Eskimo woman shaman, celebrated the joy of nature's influence on the human spirit:

> The great sea
> Has sent me adrift.
> It moves me
> as the weed in a great river.
> Earth and the great weather
> Move me
> Have carried me away
> And move my inward parts with joy.[8]

The twelfth century mystic Hildegard of Bingen has written movingly about the oneness of all creation: ". . . everything that is in the heavens, on the earth, and under the earth is penetrated with connectedness, is penetrated with relatedness. . . . God has arranged all things in the world in consideration of everything else." Cut off from the one flow of energy that quickens all living things, separated from the rhythm of universal patterns and sequences that bring balance and power, severely out of touch with the cosmic womb in which we were fashioned—it is small wonder that on the one hand our planet is ailing, if not dying, from our relentless disregard for its needs, and on the other hand we ourselves are deeply afflicted both spiritually and physically as we continue our lonely journey away from the very source of our healing and wholeness—our mother earth who alone knows how to nourish and guide us. Stories about cosmic intimacy move us deeply.

> When the moon is full and the sea swells, my sleep is restless because some surge that links the stars and the atoms washes through my body like the tide. . . . When I am tuned to the rhythms of my inspiration and expiration I remember that I am a coming together of a community of atoms. I am a little world, a microcosm. Everything that is happening anywhere in the world is happening in me. The moon rises in my blood; lilacs bloom in my nostrils; suns are born and burst in the atoms that are my substance. I am one body with the world.[9]

Under the general theme of "cosmic loneliness" I wish to include our parallel alienation from our own bodies. This too has left us in a sorry state. Even though there are many explanations for these alienations it is still almost beyond belief that we humans are so bent on self-destruction that most of us ignore or resent the last call to sanity and wholeness. By loving and befriending the body—both the tortured body of the mother earth who gave us birth and the individual and most beautiful body that is a precious part of our present and eternal future— we may still be in time to lessen the unnecessary loneliness that keeps us from enjoying the rich intimacy for which we were created.

There is a third kind of loneliness—the "loneliness of change." The mystical and cosmic awareness that we touched upon in the preceding pages often anticipate, or are the result of, personal transformation and the grace of transcendence. The transformed self is a changed self. It meets the world differently. It has a new set of values, needs, expectations, gifts and sensibilities. It makes new connections, finds deeper meaning to existence and celebrates its own originality. Every such life grows stronger, looking toward its own star. The attraction to follow that star is irresistible. There is no going back from life at the edge of the miraculous. Personal transformation of this nature is irrevocable. The chicken can never become an egg again.

I write of the "loneliness of change" because the first impact of personal transformation is on relationships; they improve or deteriorate but rarely stay the same. There are endless examples from within institutions, communities, friendships and marriages of the alienation that results from a radical transformation in one member's newly acquired life-stance. The change is usually regarded as threatening to the others. When the habits and parameters of a relationship may be perceived as preventing growth into richer, more creative self-possession, when spiritual growth becomes more desirable than material success, the partner who still supports the old agenda and who is content with the status quo is liable to feel isolated, rejected and inferior.

These personal changes are notoriously awkward to explain in a convincing manner. It either comes across as a momentary loss of sanity that rest and fresh air will cure, a desperate effort to draw attention to oneself, a passing infatuation with some long-haired New Age guru from California or a perfectly understandable indication of early (or late) mid-life crisis. There are, as yet, no acceptable categories of description such as personal development, career change, sabbatical leave, vocation and so on to provide an accurate account of the transformation. The lack of such a vocabulary serves only to increase suspicion in an already precarious bonding between people. In their most intimate relationships many people seek security and protection. They are deeply affected by fear—fear of the future, fear of loss, fear of rejection.

> If, through whatever medium—meditation, a social movement, assertiveness training, quiet reflection, a new spirituality—one partner breaks free of fear and conditioning, the relationship becomes unfamiliar territory. Reassurances help very little. The threatened partner may show open disapproval, either through anger, mockery or argument. . . . If the fearful partner cannot adjust or join, there will eventually be a rift, either actual or psychological. Those who stay in a relationship hostile to their new world have two choices: to be open about their interests, which may fuel the misunderstanding, or to become clandestine. Either way, they can no longer explore, within their relationship, the most meaningful developments in their lives.[10]

There is a great sadness at this time because of the truth that is being rejected—freedom, fulfillment, creativity. The loneliness arises from the loss of a journey together—either as a community, a staff, or a loving partner. It is futile to try to convince, to persuade, to cajole. You cannot force the river. We come to understandings and paradigm shifts in our own time and in our own ways. And each one's timing is different. Of one thing we are sure: our highest responsibility is to the development of our own potential, to be all we can, to be true to our own selves. Theodore Roszak observed that most of us are "sick with guilt at having lived below our authentic level," and Daniel Levinson remarked that much of our weeping is at the sight of the difference between who we are and what we dreamed of becoming.

It probably comes as no surprise to the reflective reader that most of the resistance to growth comes from within ourselves. We choose, often unconsciously, to block from our awareness any information or experience that implies a need for change in our deepest beliefs. And yet our deepest beliefs include the necessity for growth. Abraham Maslow identifies "the fear of knowing and the need to know." We fear the darkness within but we fear even more the beauty that lies hidden there. We resist the growing that we most deeply desire. We resist the insights that enable us to actualize our highest capabilities because they dispel the illusions that we have come to cherish so unquestioningly—the illusion, for instance, that we can be certain of "having the truth," or that we are utterly worthless.

> Low self-esteem—giving in to our resistance to excelling, living out our potential, living out what we know to be true within ourselves—is a much more comfortable route to follow . . . the fear of knowing what one is capable of doing, the anxiety that comes from doing our best and living out our potential greatness is directly connected to the fear of being responsible.[11]

Not growing is comfortable, and growing is likely to be very disturbing at times. It is stable and certain to stay put—irregular, erratic and unpredictable to grow. We also suspect that if we start being courageous in this respect, if we once begin to take risks, we will continue to do so for the rest of our lives, ". . . and others will snipe at us and we will make mistakes, and sometimes we'll make utter fools of ourselves but life will never be dull. . . ."[12]

For most of us the challenge is too great.

SUFFERING

Fuel for Growing

Sometimes we can peep through small windows into the vast mystery of suffering. At the very best one can only hope for a glimpse of meaning into what appears to be the single most distressing experience in the human condition. But is suffering an ambiguous destroyer or a mysterious blessing? And can it be avoided? There are approaches to personal growth that underplay the necessity of suffering. This is a cause for concern. I will discuss this now and then indicate that not only is necessary suffering to be tolerated and accepted but, ideally, to be welcomed and befriended. What is certain is this: if we are to grow we must suffer.

Since self-esteem is a central theme in this book, one of the first issues to be met here is the way that suffering is dealt with (or not) in most books, programs and conferences devoted to the enhancement of self-image and self-value. The pain involved in such growth seems to me to be denied in many instances, or at least underplayed. The unease I experience concerns the vagueness of any spirituality, theology or philosophy that may be called upon to support the generally accepted approach to the acquisition of self-esteem—a spirituality that would anticipate, identify and assess the many hazards and ambushes that lie in wait for the explorers who travel the pathways to self-esteem.

There is, undoubtedly, a mysterious darkness in our hearts which resists the light of truth about creation in general and about ourselves in particular. This kingdom is notoriously slow to surrender. Only with prolonged preparation and a commitment to careful strategies will the sinister sentries of the self-esteem resistance movement be outmaneuvered. With prayer, fasting and discipline of the heart we lay siege to the fortress of the shadow, or of original sin, or of whatever one terms the stubborn inner resistance to light, or to grace, or to all that tends toward the positive, the worthy, the free. What worries me is this: all efforts to present the enhancement of self-esteem, self-acceptance and all kinds of significant growth in perceptions of self-worth and self-value will result only in a deeper sense of unworthiness and therefore of depression if the perverse nature of our complicated make-up is not totally respected. The script of the human capacity for resisting growth is written in every heart. We ignore it at our peril. There is no such thing as instant self-esteem. The divorce list is long and the honeymoons are brief in most hurried "self" and "esteem" marriages.

Popular literature on self-esteem over the last three decades abounds with assumptions concerning emotional and attitudinal growth. What is most alarming is the presumption regarding unaided human potential. Insights that have taken ages to clarify about the cultivation of an appropriate self-image are often presented as though self-obvious and readily available. Habits of mind that take years of self-discipline to master are promised to those who repeat daily affirmations. Radical changes of heart, usually the fruit of prolonged meditations and study, are expected by tomorrow or by the end of the program or workshop. But there never was cheap grace, nor is there such a commodity now.

Gerald May, whose wisdom in these matters is widely respected, suggests that a wordy, psychological approach, devoid

of spirituality, forever examining explanations, reasons and mo-
tivations for self-mastery, can create *willful* people, aggressively
in pursuit of control, assertiveness and autonomy. He contrasts
such a development with a more humble and spiritual approach
to self-esteem which helps to nurture *willing* people, aware of
the mystery of self, of the wider picture of mutuality, of the
impossibility of growing alone, of patiently living out the questions while relentlessly remaining open to the wisdom and
power of the Spirit in whom all "selves" rely for their esteem.

Unaided—whether the source of power is located inside
or outside one's own self—the chances of success in the acquisition of self-esteem are rather slim. Most traditional religions
have profound respect for that persistent, stubborn and un-
tameable dimension of our human nature which is the ever-
present shadow of every facet of actual and potential growth.

The achieving of wisdom and vision, of high self-esteem, of
a courageous heart are often the special blessings with which
suffering is rewarded. The golden child within is rarely brought
to birth without a lot of pain. The "hidden self" referred to by
St. Paul will emerge only after prolonged and careful persuasion. For the Christian it is grace that enables a person to be
very aware of the labyrinth between the ideal self and the actual
self—between the way one is and the secret dreams of what one
might become.

The journey inward is beset by hazards at every turn. A
part of us has hidden the key to the deep-down secrets from
which our malaise stems. The whole business of building up
self-esteem touches on complicated dimensions of our psyches
that stir up anxiety and apprehension. Carl Jung verifies this
conviction. "Wherever there is reaching down into innermost
experience, into the nucleus of personality, most people are
overcome by fright, and many run away. . . . The risk of inner
experience, the adventure of the spirit, is, in any case, alien to
most human beings." An even deeper level of resistance is dis-

cerned by Anthony de Mello. He writes about people's fear of being healed, of being free. "Nobody wants to be healed. Clients seek only to be relieved of their symptoms, to make some little effort, to learn some tricks to try out on others, or to prove that they are beyond remedy and nobody can cure them. Rare is the person who wants to be healed, who really wants total liberation from all conditioning and is ready to take the trouble to pay the price to attain that state."[13]

In these paragraphs I am simply calling attention to what I regard as a serious omission in the rationale behind many new self-esteem programs. That omission concerns the ambiguous intricacies of the human spirit and the paradoxes of the heart when it comes to empowerment and liberation. The causes of low self-esteem stay shrouded in psychic darkness. The wounded child avoids the light. There is a history of pain to the negative self-concept. But through silence and ritual and skilled counseling the stubborn scaffolding of perennial resistance will be relentlessly dismantled. Appropriate ritual will be the pontifex for meeting the shadow, for light and darkness to play, for the wounded child to emerge and for the pain to be let out. Mourning is central here—a mourning over what has happened, over the necessary losses in life and the missed opportunities, over the irreversibility of the past. "If the pain remains inside," Matthew Fox reminds us, "rancid terror results and with it sentimentalism, violence and the stifling of creativity. Only when the pain is out can the creativity flow to do something with the pain." These reflections are offered only to provide a loving warning for all those in pursuit of elusive self-esteem so that their eventual discovery will be a lasting one.

The more clearly we see, the more we suffer. The sharper the focus the sharper the pain. An image that comes up for me is my bedroom window at home in Ireland. As the morning mists clear up I can see more clearly what the early sun illuminates during the dawn chorus—the ever-expanding parish graveyard.

Growth and grief, beginnings and endings, are the most unlikely bedfellows. Yet they need each other to keep creating,
healing and rejoicing. How unfamiliar we are with concepts
such as the power of pain, the energy within healthy tensions,
the potential of conflict. How difficult it is to suffer in a
conscious and creative manner, to lean toward the pain, to celebrate the scars. Yet all our great stories are about wounded
healers, about the heroine's journey through the night, about
the crucified saviors of humanity.

The fables, legends and myths of the world are rich with
insights into the befriending and transcendence of suffering.
Reflect for a moment on a fairy tale you remember from childhood. Such stories contain all we need to know about the mystery of suffering. Reflect also on the religious narratives of the
revealed faiths. In the Torah, for instance, the heroes of the
Jewish tradition are tested and challenged in the extreme before
the experience of redemption. In the Koran the question is
asked: "Do you think that you shall enter the Garden of Bliss
without such trials as came to those who passed before you?"
Christians will be familiar with the powerful symbols of suffering and death that forever lie at the heart of their worship. The
crushed grapes, the dying seed, the broken bread, the ubiquitous cross—all point to the centrality of vulnerability, pain and
death if individuation, freedom and resurrection are to be
experienced.

A healthy sense of the true self requires a certain familiar-
ity with pain. It is when they are close to their pain that the poor
are powerful. It is because they were in touch with their shadow
that Jesus Christ could empower the sinners, the emotionally
wounded, the oppressed women—the *anawim* of the time.
Nothing has changed. Nor has our sight improved. We cannot
understand how the wounded of the earth carry within them
the true vision of creation. Why do we sense, in a confused
manner, the explosive strength of children, of handicapped peo-

ple, of the oppressed ethnic minorities throughout the world? What instinct alerts us to the hidden beauty in the neglected and rejected? And whose pleading voice reminds us that when we burn our suffering as fuel for our spirit, our pristine loveliness is once again disclosed?

It is for these reasons that creation spirituality advocates a coming-to-terms with our unease, a befriending of our pain, a recognition of the hidden richness of suffering. The mystics trust the darkness, participate in the silence, identify with winter and go with the flow of grief, anger and outrage.

> Experience the pain. Let us not fear its impact on ourselves or others. We will not shatter, for we are not objects that can break. Nor will we get stuck in this pain for it is dynamic, it flows through us. Drop our defenses. Let us stay present to its flow, express it—in words, movements and sounds.[14]

There is a cosmic reality about our personal pain. Even infinite love was not spared suffering. Who will tell us about the networking of pain throughout the universe? Who knows of the healing brought about when the trapped energy of suffering is set free by the dark physician? How do we measure the compassion, redemption, and liberation that flood the countryside of our hearts and of the cosmos when the divine energy locked up in buried-alive pain is released on its life-giving way? What must we do to begin living like this, to become part of this wider way of being?

In good ritual there is a pattern that connects the scattered fragments of experience into new shapes of meaning. When the symbols of a living liturgy are infused with a cosmic as well as with a community dimension, there is swift healing. Darkness and silence, for instance, endeavor to unite the suffering that echoes between the human heart, the heart of humanity and the very cosmic heart itself.

People who cannot share their cosmic pain cannot worship together. Worship is the emptying of all we have, and pain and suffering are deep within us all. In worship among black people or native peoples pain is not covered up. It is spoken out, it is chanted out, it is sung out, it is danced out. In short it is connected to the rest of our lives and to the universe itself. Simone Weil advises us to return all suffering to the universe.[15]

In the bread and wine of the eucharist—the earth's harvest and the artistry of human hands—grief, for the Christian, is transcended into power. Through unity and solidarity with the agony of Jesus Christ the suffering of the world is transformed. Only cosmic symbols can celebrate the healing and creativity at the heart of universal lamentation.

SUMMARY

Identifying Low Self-Esteem

1. Powerlessness

<u>Power is given away</u>. It must be reclaimed. Women surrender their power to men; men to institutions; all to the authoritarianism of the mass media with its agenda of consumerism and doctrinal propaganda. Has *your* power been given away? Power and energy are reclaimed by reconnecting with the source of life and love. How does one prevent the drainage of the flow of power?

There are toxic people who can weaken us, who can absorb our energy. Until we are stronger, they are to be avoided. We are encouraged to pray for them: we are not obliged to be in their company. We befriend those who empower us: they come to nurture us when we need them like a straying spring day in the middle of February.

2. Feelings of Inferiority

A severe sense of inadequacy accompanies low self-esteem; there is an inability to self-assert. Outwardly cool and collected, most people feel inadequate. Inferiority feelings are at the root of many personality difficulties and phobias. "Not good enough" is a shockingly common slogan. Alfred Adler, the

Austrian psychologist, claims that everyone has a problem with such feelings. Many overcompensate by boasting.

It is difficult to change such an attitude. Centering prayer, affirmations, and avoidance of comparisons are some of the strategies suggested in this book for opening new windows onto more confident living.

3. Guilt Feelings and Anxiety

Those with low self-esteem will often reveal that they not only hate their sins but themselves as sinners. They feel unlovable in their own eyes and in the eyes of God. We can see this in ourselves and others. There are different kinds of guilt—unconscious guilt, false guilt—leading to continual overreaction and overcompensation, to the persistent desire to punish oneself, e.g. the exaggerated feeling of responsibility for a parent's death without reason.

There is a great need for such people to forgive themselves; this is often more difficult than forgiving others. At this point projection is common and the following characteristics develop.

4. A Tendency To Judge and Condemn

Guilt is then projected onto others. Low self-esteemers tend to be harsh on themselves as a result of perfectionism. Identifiable efforts are made to disguise negative attitudes—e.g. "I don't want to be critical but . . ."—followed by an emotional assassination. A feature of this condition is the holding of unreasonable expectations.

Again, the grace of self-forgiveness must be sought after—and an understanding of the "art of the possible." Self-knowledge is so important here to discern the patterns that form within us, such as the habit of constant fault-finding and carping criticism.

5. *Difficulties in Receiving Thanks or Praise*

Compliments are not really accepted or owned at the emotional level; they are deflected, e.g. "A pure fluke ..."; "You caught me on a good day ..." etc. A false humility and a false worry about appearing proud lead to a focus on one's failures and an unhealthy reluctance to take responsibility for one's talents.

Some people must learn to appreciate each affirmation with grace, e.g. "Thank you. I deserve it."

6. *Reluctance To Ask for Help*

This reluctance often stems from a fear of refusal. There is also a tendency to refuse help: "It's O.K. I can manage by myself" = "I'm not worth your time." And the difficulty in saying "no" to others does not always arise from generosity as from a desire to please, to be accepted. "I'll only be liked for what I do, not for what I am."

A true humility and sense of reality is needed. The inverted self-deprecation must be revealed for what it is—a false self-evaluation.

7. *Exaggerated Fear of Failure*

Low self-esteemers can only identify with success. They are often workaholics suffering from "burn-out" and haunted by a fear of failure. Oversensitive about other people's opinions, they are frequently unable to handle, acknowledge or befriend their negative feelings, e.g. anger, outrage and fear.

A new attitude toward failure is possible, e.g. there is no such thing as failure, only valuable experience and delay. Every failure is an opportunity to grow, depending on our point of view. Samuel Smiles wrote that we learn wisdom from failure much more than from success. "We often find out what will do by finding out what will not do, and probably those who never made a mistake never made a discovery." Therefore risks are both necessary and difficult to take.

8. Feelings of Jealousy and Envy

There are times when we are all ambivalent about three-way relationships. Jealousy is usually linked with insecurity and poor self-image, envy from unnecessary comparisons with others, leading to resentment and aggression.

Comparisons of this kind are useless and counterproductive. But our negative feelings can be maximized into growth. I can deal constructively with suspicion and frustration. When an oyster is irritated it makes a pearl. Trust and generosity of spirit can also grow from stifling attitudes.

9. Difficulties in Trusting

When one cannot trust the self, trust in others becomes impossible. We are haunted by the ubiquitous fear of rejection. "Why am I afraid to tell you who I am?" "I will only let you see that side of me that is acceptable to you." Therefore I must not reveal my deeper feelings. I must remember to stay full of caution and take no chances.

This is a crucial point: without trust there can be no growth, no letting go, no self-esteem. Love always makes us vulnerable, so we must become vulnerable. The amazing story of incarnation can be heard in the light of God's unique risk in becoming defenseless before evil.

10. Addictions Connected with Low Self-Esteem

Many of the emotionally wounded live lives of quiet desperation. There is the perennial escape into tranquillizers, sleeping pills, eating compulsively, gambling, and becoming TV addicts. This can only lead to self-contempt, and a dangerous downward spiral is created. We disintegrate: our energy drains away.

A beginning is needed—one firm foothold, one strong hand, one clear warning. Then we begin to move.

11. *Tendencies to Stress-Related Illness*

Negative feelings are very stressful; anxiety, guilt, envy, and irrational fear are very destructive. The mess our hearts get into, the daily conflicts with ourselves, withheld forgiveness—all make life an uphill struggle with more dark than light. The body's defenses are lowered and illness becomes more likely. It has been well established by the medical profession that sixty percent of all sickness and disease is due to psychosomatic causes. Centering prayer, relaxation techniques, open communication with friends—all are necessities here if we are to become less vulnerable to stress.

12. *Negative Images of God*

People with poor self-images tend to project their negative attitudes on God, seeing him as they see themselves, e.g. in a judgmental way. They feel the need to appease him, especially if they suffer from morbid guilt. Unaware of their inner glory they are blind to God's glory too. They cannot grow out of the male images of a tough God imprinted on their hearts in childhood.

13. *An Attitude of Protectiveness about Possessions*

This attitude can apply to almost anything, including material things, time or ideas. The price for this acquisitiveness is high; there is a resulting lack of peace in hanging on to things, and in worry about losing them or in anxiety about others bene-fiting from them. But we do not grow by acquiring more, only by letting go. "We grow by subtraction," preached Meister Eckhart. All that is let go is given to myself.

With appropriate music and a positive frame of mind, the following meditation may help you to discern the hidden pres-sures in your life, and help you to identify what aspects of rela-tionships or what attitudes might be "let go of" if your spiritual growth is to continue.

14. Guided Imagery for a "Letting Go" Meditation

(Begin with the usual suggestions about breathing, posture, awareness, relaxation and openness to the Spirit of love.)

You are walking on wet swampy ground. It is a stormy day. You are laden with baggage—two heavy suitcases in your hands, bags on your back—and you are struggling against the wind. Your overcoat is too heavy; your shoes are too loose and now full of water.

You are feeling weak and sweaty and very anxious. Your heart is weary and your mind is spinning. You feel yourself sinking in the mud, overwhelmed by the conditions, trying to remain upright by grasping at the branches of a wildly sway-ing tree.

The water is rising now, up to your knees, pushing hard against you and you are losing your balance. Your possessions are slipping from your grasp. You are full of panic. The water is getting higher and the wind is blowing stronger. You are on the point of collapse. The muddy water is up to your waist. The threshing branch is whipped from your grasp. You stumble, you stagger, you scream as you collapse.

At that moment you let go of all your belongings—bags,

branches, suitcases, overcoat and shoes. Everything is let go on the swirling waves. So let them go . . . let them go now. Abandon yourself to the elements and trust the water. Suddenly you are floating. You feel light and buoyant, free and flowing, firmly and lovingly supported as you float on your back on a calm, calm lake. The sun is warm on your face. Feel the warmth as it graces, soothes and blesses your body. Everything is so different . . . and beautiful.

　　You are at peace . . . at peace . . .

Third Window

The Wonder of Healing

CREATIVITY

God's Need of Our Passion

The mystic will be no stranger to the mystery of the tension at the roots of the spirit where these elemental forces encounter each other—the allurement toward freedom with its certain risks and the grip of the status quo with its promise of security. The creation spirituality of the mystic emphasises the unique place of the *via negativa* in the development of the spirit. Its unique insight into this dark mystery of seemingly conflicting energies helps us to seek resolution and growth more in terms of engagement and transcendence rather than in confrontation and submission, in befriending rather than in overcoming, so that the *via creativa* may be birthed *in* the heart of darkness and not *after* the darkness has passed, because that is not the way the mystery of life unfolds. We need the mystic to remind us of this. It is the mystic in each of us that urges us to dance with the pain of the "dark night of the soul" rather than to deny its reality; to enter into the rhythm of the resistance we experience rather than to attack it; to *be with* the emptiness rather than to fill it too soon.

The Christian revelation sheds much needed light on this mysterious paradox. The creation tradition points to the chaos that preceded the first loving creation of the universe twenty billion years ago, and the darkness two thousand years ago that accompanied the creation of the Christian era. From the beginning and forever, the light of creativity and the resistance of darkness co-exist in tension—the tension that awakens the inner artist to fashion new expressions in color, shape, sound and movement, especially in the context of the routine patterns of life. Because we are created in the creator's image, we are already and always graced with a co-creative role in the transformation of mother earth into the new creation.

This awesome responsibility will usually be exercised in the shadow context of suffering. Meister Eckhart reminds us that "we are heirs of the fearful creative power of God." This is the inheritance of everyone, not just the celebrated artists. God's incarnate presence is revealed as creativity. This flowing presence enlivens and sustains all of life. It keeps the grass growing, the tides rolling and the planets turning. Humans, too, uniquely share in this sacred energy and each person is a special kind of artist. Were it not for his mother, Pablo Casals, the musical genius, could easily have been a carpenter. He had a fine reverence for all kinds of artisans.

> I have always regarded manual labor as creative and looked with respect—and, yes, wonder—at people who work with their hands. It seems to me that their creativity is no less than that of a violinist or a painter. It is of a different sort, that is all.[1]

And despite the negativities—indeed, as we have seen, because of them—the creative passion flourishes and the *via negativa* is transcended. The shell of pain must be cracked before the energy within can be released. The heart must be broken so that at the point of fracture the power of the artist can emerge. When the resistance is befriended the creative force is deepened and the *via creativa* is entered. At this moment in a person's life—a moment that has no chronological parameters—there are many identifiable characteristics and emotions. Fused with the resistance and pain, a deep joy and passion fill the heart. There is also play and imagination, and lots of trust. Through the third window let us have a glance at some of these graces.

If there is no joy it is not the divine artist at work. The hallmark of the one who is creating is delight.

> God is our creator. God made us in his image and likeness. Therefore we are creators. He gave us a garden to till and cultivate. We became co-creators by our responsible acts, whether in bringing forth children, or producing food, furniture or clothing. The joy of creativeness should be ours.[2]

This joy is missing from so many hearts. But there is more than joy in the face of our ever-creating Mother God, eternally birthing what is new and beautiful. There is delight and passion too. It was sacred passion that led to creation in the first place so that the intimacy of incarnation could happen later in time but first in intention. It was the burning passion of a God that assumed the vulnerability of a baby and experienced the ecstasy and the agony of an extraordinarily ordinary human being. It is with this passion that we, in turn, are graced as co-creators with God in loving our universe forward into a garden of Eden where fear and death are forever forgotten. It is as though God has revealed to us in the incarnation that he has locked his creative passion into human hearts and that the world cannot evolve further until we discover these divine powers within. God and his creation are waiting for us to admit our responsibility and to realize our unique role in the scheme of things. Because of misleading education and mistaken theology, our self-understanding has been seriously flawed, and as a consequence our self-esteem is appallingly low. A fuller acceptance of the powerful beauty of our spirit in hastening in the age of love will inspire in us a passion for the possible, bestowing and establishing an unsurpassing dignity on both humanity and all creation.

As with joy and passion, play and imagination are central to creativity in thought and deed. There was a divine playfulness in the creation of the world when God and wisdom delighted in what they were doing.

> I was by his side, a master artist,
> delighting him day after day,
> ever at play in his presence,
> at play everywhere in the world,
> delighting to be with the children of men.[3]

This playfulness continues today in the continually sustaining love of her in whom we smile and dance and throw parties. It is the same, therefore, with us who, graced with such divine love, are called to co-create with God.

> Every good idea and all creative work are the offspring of the imagination, and have their source in what one is pleased to call childhood fantasy. Not the artist alone but every creative individual owes all that is greatest in his or her life to fantasy. . . . Without this playing with fantasy no creative work has ever yet come to birth.[4]

The link between true humanity and play comes to mind here as does the importance of childhood qualities in adulthood. If to be creative is of the essence of the fully alive person and if creativity is about playing, then we are not surprised at how essential it is for all of us to discover, nurture and delight in the child within us. This beautiful, divine child may well be a wounded one, and the wounds will have a deadly effect on the quality and quantity of our joy-filled creativity. But in the healing the inspiration returns. Baudelaire remarked that the artist's creative power is released when he or she establishes a healthy bond with the child in the heart. I mentioned trust as a discernible dimension of creativity. As I will suggest later in this third "window," trust is a necessary fundamental attitude for human growth in love and hope. Erik Erikson describes the primal relationship of the child as "basic trust." Without it there can be no exploring, inventiveness or even discovery. Since the young child is not clear about differences, this basic trust is placed in the mother, in the world, in the cosmos itself. This trust is later identifiable as central to the artist's and the mystic's reliance on experience—a trust in what happens, in how we interpret what happens, in how we express that interpretation. In other words there can be no creativity without trust in one's self, in others, in the universe, in God. Otherwise we are hopelessly adrift on a sea of suspicion. Instead of perceiving experience as gift and as gracious, we regard what happens to us as confrontation and as threatening. The beginnings of neurosis can often be traced back to the sowing of these seeds in the young heart in the name of education, religion or life-skills.

> The neurotic's problem at bottom is . . . an inability to affirm. . . . The neurotic cannot affirm himself—and therefore he is at war with himself. He cannot affirm his situation among his fellows—and so he regards them with suspicion and hostility. And finally, the neurotic cannot affirm life as a whole; he cannot affirm the universe. . . . Inability to affirm is merely another term for inability to trust.[5]

I now want to draw these reflections together by making a brief link between the four steps of an emerging creativity and the four windows or paths of creation spirituality. The first step is about paying attention to our dreams and our sense of wonder. There is an unconscious dynamic at work, shaping for us in visions and fantasy, the potential of the spirit, as cosmic, human and personal. Creativity begins with an awareness of how wonderful these possibilities are—an awareness that is nurtured and developed by attentiveness, carefulness and trust. In creation spirituality this flow of loving power is perceived as the creative energy of God incarnate—an energy forever reaching toward actualization. This reaching—the *via positiva*—is experienced as desire, commitment, or, as Puccini put it, an awareness of one's "soul-force." "Then," he continued, "I feel the burning desire and intense resolve to create something worthwhile."[6]

Once the subconscious is "contacted" and the emotional concentration is fed into the underground river of creativity, a period of "letting go" is necessary. The mystics call it the *via negativa*. Rudyard Kipling writes about befriending your demon who may be the leader on this path. ". . . do not try to think consciously. Drift, wait, and obey." This is a time of silence, of a certain kind of emptiness during which "incubation" takes place. "At a certain stage in every creation, preparation ceases, and the ingredients have to be left to "cook" in order to allow the subconscious to operate on the problem." That is how the creation technician would put it. The mystic would probably offer images of inner conflict and painful resistance from which the harmony emerges and the loss is transformed into growth.

A third discernible step in the process of creativity is that of "breakthrough" or "illumination" or "emergence"—sometimes sudden, sometimes slow. Tchaikovsky writes about the germ of a future composition. "It takes root with extraordinary force and shoots up through the earth, puts forth branches and leaves, and finally blossoms. I cannot define the creative process in any other way. . . ." The *via creativa* is when the way ahead is clear, when the melody is heard, when the beauty is visible. Creation spirituality recognizes the healing and the ecstasy of this "moment" of wholeness and growth, of a deepened presence, of connecting and returning and spreading. The inner spring of divine newness is tapped (maybe in the desert) and the flow of life-giving images and sounds and tangible beauty blesses our waiting hearts.

> The great secret of all creative geniuses is that they possess the power to appropriate the beauty, the wealth, the grandeur, and the sublimity within their own souls, which are a part of Omnipotence, and to communicate those riches to others.[7]

In their rather technical approach to "higher creativity," Harman and Rheingold offer the principle of verification as the fourth and final step in the creative process. Put more simply, the question might be asked: "Does it work?" or "Is it catching on?" or "Are things changing for the better because of the breakthrough?" The mystics wrote about the *via transformativa*. Creative healing will bring about social transformation. The inner growing anticipates the compassion that works toward universal justice and peace. That is why our personal daily moments of breakthrough are so important.

> The action of the child inventing a new game with his playmates; Einstein formulating a theory of relativity; the housewife devising a new sauce for the meat; a young author writing his first novel; all of these are, in terms of our definition, creative, and there is no attempt to set them in some order of more or less creative.[8]

The ultimate creative process, however, will be centered around the renewal of the face of the earth, where the universal dream of all humanity and all creation from the beginning of time and before will come true. How will this come about? In a world where militarism and consumerism are so intrinsic to the texture of daily life, what hope is there of a change of heart? There is a shadow of racism in every heart, a pull toward domi-

nation and even violence in every human psyche. Can these
elemental forces be transcended? Can the mutilation of our
beloved mother earth be stopped in time? In *The Coming of the
Cosmic Christ* Matthew Fox makes a suggestion:

> I believe the answer lies in a deep mystical awakening the
> likes of which the planet has never witnessed before—a
> mystical awakening that is truly planetary, that draws out
> the wisdom and the mystic, the player and the justice-
> maker from the wisdom traditions of all religions and cul-
> tures. Such a mystical awakening would surely birth that
> "peace on earth" for which creation longs—the promise
> given two thousand years ago in Bethlehem.[9]

RECOGNIZING

The Hidden Love Story

Ecstatic! No other word was appropriate for describing the fervor with which they embraced. The nuptial mass had just been celebrated, and the radiant young woman and young man were about to begin the always-new journey down the aisle, deeply delighted with themselves and with each other. So were the guests on either side who smiled and clapped and clicked their cameras. Shortly the local community would be alerted to the fact that a wedding was taking place, when the cavalcade of shiny cars with flowing streamers would toot-toot its way along the winding road by the hills, into Killarney. As I watched this healthy, fulfilled couple, strolling dreamily down through the church, acknowledging the admiration of their friends while the organist excelled herself, something very significant crossed my mind. It was the awareness of God's delight at what was happening.

Each person there had a different reason for being happy, from the parents of the newlyweds to myself who had just wandered in "for a visit" on this bright day at the end of a gray week. God, however, was delighted because in the passion and praise of that fine moment, when human love reached out in risk to commit itself in trust to a whole lifetime of living, he knew again that his grand plan was supremely successful. Let me explain what I mean. When God, at the very beginning, having created a most beautiful world full of flora and fauna, created human beings who would love each other enough to spend a lifetime together, he was simply beginning a process that would last forever and end only when nothing but love remained.

This is the first and only love story. It is the seminal plot of every subsequent romance throughout the ages. Overwhelmed by her own passion, God gave birth to all creation, pouring her love and beauty into the shapes and sounds and seeds that we call the world. At the height of her artistry, trusting her imagination in its finest hour, she fashioned human beings with the capacity to fall in love with each other and thus perpetuate the very creative energy—her own divine longing—that brought about the universe in the first place. And just as the cosmos, the world and humanity can be seen as God's first child, the fruit of her love, so too every baby born of love is another incarnation of the creator's passion. As perennial as the grass, new love would continue to bring bright hope.

As the couple moved slowly outside into the brown light of November sunshine, I became acutely aware of a breathtaking mystery unfolding around me. It was God himself who was celebrating in the sacramental moment of bonding. Incarnate, he *was* the human love that had leaped, like a spark, from heart to heart, starting yet another flame, to spread, in this small place on the verge of the mighty Atlantic, the warmth of an eternal lover. This morning's moment was a triumph for the sacred heart of divine creativity. It was the vindication of God's folly in entrusting his future to the vulnerable ambiguity of the human condition. Here, I reflected, was hope for a world grown cynical from disillusionment about love's promises. Here, too, was healing for a world always hurting from the daily pain of broken dreams.

The celebrating community of joy had now moved away and I sat in the empty church busy with my thoughts. Within a few minutes the pews were filling up again. The atmosphere was already different. I looked at the people. Most of them were either very old or very handicapped. They shuffled, stumbled, swayed to their places. Some limped, some were carried, many were pushed. Unlike the rest of us, they carried their wounds on the outside. There they were, God's special branch, the *anawim* of the community, arriving in good time for a cere-mony of blessing. In contrast to the colorful vignette of a com-munity rejoicing an hour ago, here was the somber picture of a community suffering. Quietly, sometimes confused, sometimes cheerful, they moved carefully on to the confetti-sprinkled pews. I sensed a pain and power as the frail and damaged bodies obediently reached their appointed places.

I reflected on this other face of the community and, there-fore, another face of the incarnate God—the weeping face. Over the years my image of the omnipotent and unchanging God had gradually given way to a God who loved with a human heart, who cried salty tears and who experienced everything that is to be experienced of human agony and ecstasy. Today that compassionate God was not merely reaching to these brave sisters and brothers from the outside, giving extra grace to sup-port them until death would bring a happy release from their exile down here. No, just as earlier in the day God was incarnate in the ecstatic joy of a couple in love, thoroughly enjoying him-self in the experience of risking, trusting and letting go in the commitment of marriage, so too he is now deeply inside the perfect hearts of these outwardly afflicted people, identifying with their pain, their courage, their anxieties and their hope. It is God who is suffering in this human distress; it is God who is desperately yearning for a more abundant life for these, his human images, the special children of his womb. It is the lust for life of God that lifts the morning eyelid of a hurting body to another aching day of pain. And when the evening comes, no beating drums are there to welcome home the lonely heart, no cheering crowds acclaim the silent victories of spirit. But God is there, touching from inside, the tired eyes of doubt until they shine again and sparkle in the quiet celebration of the heart.

Daniel Dancing Fish once said to me that the most beautiful things about God, when fleshed into time, space and humanity, emerge as suffering. Why this is so will ultimately remain mysterious. Even though we catch all kinds of glimpses into the meaning of the mystery, at best we see but darkly. What happened at the incarnation sheds some light. It was from the heart of the deepest agony in the man Jesus Christ that the most explosive and redemptive energy ever released powered its way throughout the length and breadth of the cosmos. From that highly charged disclosure point that we call redemption or salvation or new creation it follows, I believe, that there is a divine and astonishing beauty behind every pain. Some know, accept and own that revelation, and become saints, proclaimed or not. Others stop growing. As I watched and wondered at the inner conflicts of the sick and handicapped as they humbly and gratefully acknowledged the blessing of the church I realized how blessed they already were, consecrated on their own altars of pain, living sacrifices of praise.

It is true that the local wedding was marked by much finery, food and festivity and that the tone for the gathering of the elderly and the sick was more restrained and reflective. Yet both the morning celebration and the afternoon blessing had much in common. Each was a window of wonder on the amazing implications of incarnation. The limitlessness of God's love, for instance, was evident in such a strikingly new way as God himself rejoiced in the adventure of human love, and, in the community of those who were differently-abled, his compassion was set free to continue the work of saving them from their anxiety and despair. On both occasions the Spirit of the risen Christ, enfleshed forever among us, was sanctifying and healing the world. These truths of creation spirituality I believed with all my strength as I tried to meditate at the back of the church that autumn day. Insights such as these about the divine love and meaning at the center of the cosmos and in the tiniest cell were precious morsels for my hungry heart.

Throughout this reflection I have been using the marriage and healing ceremonies as windows through which we catch a glimpse of what God's love is *like*. Let me now go beyond that and submit to you that human ecstasy, devotion, commitment, service, healing, hurting actually *is* the incarnate God, *is* the spirit of the risen Christ deeply within, rejoicing and weeping in human hearts with their nights and mornings, their seasons of change. Why does this surprise us? Have we not always been told that God became human, pervading every aspect of our thoughts and feelings, purifying, sanctifying and completing every smile and every tear, every hope and every endeavor. Deep in our spirits it is the love of God that empowers us to be brave in the face of deadening pain, crippling anxiety or numbing routine, to be freely forgiving even as the river flows, to be trusting in a conspiracy of deceit, to stay loving even when the others have stopped.

But how do we know that this story is true? We don't. We trust. Our hearts are coded for trusting. We are graced from the beginning with a readiness for believing, for hearing the word of that story. We listen and believe because it is Christ who tells the story. It is Christ, in fact, who *is* the story. The Christian sees the hidden love and meaning of God's stunning plans in all life-experiences because these amazing designs were revealed, in the first place, in the humanity of Jesus Christ. There is nothing more calculated to keep us in a perpetual state of wonder than the possibility of catching glimpses of the changing face of God, now smiling, now serious, now silent, now playing, in all the events of life. It can, in fact, take up one's whole attention. It entails a double kind of looking, a second level of apprehension. You become aware of what is going on around you, and then of what is going on within that. In one sense you release your focus at the first level of perception so that you can venture not around or above or beside what you are watching or hearing or touching but somehow *within* the experience. It is a kind of sixth sense that helps to translate the so-called ordinary into a magic window of wonder and surprise. What happens, I think, is that a very deep, intimate, and most authentic part of us recognizes this formerly hidden landscape as the true country of our infinite spirit and everything else seems, by comparison, quite unreal or even counterfeit. Addictions and most of the usual attachments and attractions seem to lose their hold on our hearts as we try to keep ourselves in readiness for the next opportunity to stand at a window of wonder. It is not, however, always easy to be at the place with the lovely view, as T.S. Eliot well knew:

> . . . to apprehend the point of intersection of the timeless
> with time, is an occupation for the saint—no occupation
> either, but something given and taken, in a lifetime's death
> in love, ardour, and selflessness and self-surrender.[10]

How did I know that the young human passion at the altar of the church before noon, and in the altar of two loving hearts for years, was God's own love incognito? How did I discern, a short while later on that same day, the divine tears disguised as human ones on the furrowed faces of so many troubled parishioners? Because in Christ, God has revealed this to be so. Incarnation is the key to God's address—it is in his creation, but especially in humanity, that God has wished, from all time, to be known and needed, to be befriended and loved, to be admired and worshiped. It is his delight to be seen and touched and heard through the medium of the beautiful bodies that he designed, created, and, as was his desire from the beginning, eventually became. And, in becoming human, God became vulnerable—as vulnerable, in fact, as a baby; as vulnerable as two young people committing, forever, their everything to each other's keeping; as vulnerable as sick, old people waiting to be helped. With all its risk and pain, God assumed the total human condition, bestowing upon it redemptive power. Because every aspect of human life was fully experienced by God in Christ, from the ecstasy of personal transfiguration to the agony of the Calvary despair, there is no genuine human experience which is not already consecrated and empowered, redeemed and made redemptive.

To sum up, it is my deeply held conviction that God's heart beats in ours, that his spirit is the very life of ours, that he needs us to transform the world because he cannot reach others except through us, that we are God to each other, graced with unbelievable responsibility in co-creating daily with him. By virtue of incarnation, God became vulnerable; he has committed his sight to the eyes of humanity, his voice to our tongues, his hearing to our ears, and his tangibility to our bodies. In other words, God is creating and redeeming the world every day through the medium of our experiences. When we are open to be changed utterly into our true selves—the perfect images of God—the harmony that is heaven is clearly heard. We are now trapped by beauty and nothing will ever be the same again.

PRAYER

Where the Spirit Plays

The world in which we live is an ever-open, ever-new window of wonder on the delightful play of our tremendous lover, on the love and meaning that underlie everything human. It is this overwhelming insight that guides the following explorations into the personal and intimate experience called prayer.

1

(a) If every moment is a moment of grace, then prayer may be seen as a *listening* time—a listening with the heart: a quietening of our minds in stillness so that others can see themselves reflected in us with perfect clarity. Another image of prayer would be the clearing away from the floor of our hearts the pebbles, splinters and nails of jealousy and bitterness so that God and his family can walk barefoot across it to embrace.

(b) If every moment is a moment of grace, then prayer may be seen as a time of *readiness*. This preparedness, this anticipation, is to participate in the continuing revelation that every minute is. There is a condition of lightness and balance that looks expectantly at every new mountain, at every new failure, and above all at every boring routine and ordinary daily occurrence. This readiness for "I know not what" is the necessary condition for surprise and transcendence. It is the sensitivity to mystery, to the graced moment, that is the occupation of the saint.

(c) As we experience life in general as gracious gift rather than strict threat, our *images* of God will change. We will be moved at the compassion of a weeping God, the healing of an anxious God, the wisdom of a feminine God, the humor of a creating God, and the joy of an extravagant God. The image of God as a little girl or boy will speak strongly to the wounded and divine child that we all carry within us, calling to it gently but unceasingly to come out to play.

(d) If every moment is a graced moment, as incarnational theology has insisted upon from the beginning, then prayer may be regarded as an *exploration* into the experiences and the feelings that went with them, a replay of the recent or distant drama that is part of our lives, an examination of *consciousness* and basic attitudes, a *searching, finding, gathering, and connecting* of the scattered and forgotten (but maybe very significant) fragments that litter the floor of each day.

2

(a) During prayer-time, whether this is seen as a set-aside period of the day or the manner in which we are present to all our experiences at all times, *the mystic within* is awake and aware. Sometimes our mystic is present to what is happening all around, looking outward for the rich content of meditation. At other times the focus is inward, exploring the fertile mystery of the inner treasure. In either case a discipline of solitude is established before these windows, one on the universe, one on the heart, will yield their golden vistas. This solitude, this inner quality of presence, this careful distancing, is not a withdrawal from involvement. On the contrary, it is a strategy for deeper communion with the world, with others and with the self. "It is in deeper solitude," a mystic wrote, "that I find the gentleness with which I can truly love my sisters and brothers." Sometimes the more alone we are, the more pure is our affection for others —we become aware of something approaching reverence. Let me briefly outline here three areas of contemplation where the focus is, so to speak, directed through the outward window.

Many will be familiar with the exercise of developing a deep awareness of the body—our beating heart, our filling lungs, our limbs and muscles, our skin contact with clothes, chair, ground; the sounds from near and far, the smells. "Lose your mind and come to your senses." For most people these are deeply liberating moments that set crippled spirits free to dance.

Another fertile source of energy through contemplative awareness is the communion with the environment. To be in the presence of nature in a receptive and respectful manner is to be on the brink of a breakthrough. To be in a state of readiness for cosmic blessings is already to be blessed. The sky with its own life, the earth with its ageless endurance, the wind with its wisdom, the flora and fauna that perfectly reflect the glory of God, all empower us with their glad gifts to the extent that we can receive them.

Then there is the conspiracy of love, networked around the world, to channel the boundless, explosive force of human friendship into a transforming miracle. By positively identifying the people who love us and by becoming receptive to the flow of that love, we can focus and further channel it as appropriate. The potential for transformation here is of the highest order. Is it true what the visionary de Chardin said, that if we could but truly befriend the energies of love and suffering, our world, in an instant, would be transformed.

(b) The inner mystic here is at the point of stillness at the center, as Julian of Norwich put it. In the Hindu story about God's game of hide-and-seek with human beings he is advised to hide in the human heart. "There," he is told, "they will never find you." Karl Rahner identifies the activity of the Holy Spirit as the last depth and radical meaning of all that the created person experiences, enacts and suffers in the process of realizing himself as a person. ". . . when someone learns to be silent and in this inner silence lets the evil in his heart die rather than spread outward; in a word, wherever someone lives as he would like to live, combating his own egoism and the continual temptation to inner despair—there is the place of the Spirit."[11] And there too is the point toward which the inner journey is guided. We have no choice. "What is going on in your innermost being," Rainer Maria Rilke wrote in *Letters to a Young Poet*, "is worthy of your whole love." Our quest is for the underground river which is the sweep of God through all creation but especially through the human heart. Each one's mystic follows the many unnamed and unfamiliar streams that in their own time and way will joyfully merge with the divine river of life.

3

A dimension of creation-centered praying has to do with *living in the now*. This is a phrase to describe what happens when letting go becomes second nature to someone. It involves a participation in the immediacy of God, in the "nowness" of the hills and the trees. It is what happens when all is stripped away and one is reduced to the bare essentials. What is left is both ugly and beautiful but it is the real you, unencumbered by baggage. "Progress in prayer," wrote Thomas Merton, "is a continual burning of bridges behind us." Liberated from the prison of anxieties about past and future, and trusting blindly in the unconditional love that is forever springing up inside us, we are astonished at the unlimited space that is available in the now. There is no limit to what can happen in the now because it is somehow free of time. The "now" is sacred time, God's time.

When we let go in prayer we find that the present moment is never intolerable, that the pain is bearable, that maybe it can be befriended and its energy transcended. The point of power, it is said, is in the present moment. What does this mean? It means we are free to be. Our center of gravity is precisely where we are at any given moment. The past has no control over us. The future is in our hands. In a sense we decide our own future each moment by our choice of thoughts. We are redeemed from the rut, saved from the downward spiral, graced with a wonderful revelation about our capacities to shape our own destiny.

4

An elegant *simplicity* colors our lives as a consequence of living in the now, a skill that must be practiced at every moment of every day. There is a tendency in humanity toward a confusing complexity in matters spiritual. Prayer is about loving intimacy and not to be complicated by distracting regulations, liturgical deviations, and an absence of silence. The trappings, techniques and strategies surrounding prayer may, however, sometimes succeed in being a means to an end but are to be dropped the moment that spirits meet. We think again of Meister Eckhart's succinct piece of wisdom: we grow by subtraction.

I have an image of a harp on a hill, its strings full of dead leaves and stray bits of brown grass and weeds. A stiff wind is blowing. Everytime I remove a leaf, the sound of the strings, vibrating in the breeze, changes and becomes more tuneful.

Finally, with the removal of the last attachment, a melody of ecstasy echoes over the countryside. With the removal of distractions and clinging things, we are alert to the tunes of reality.

5

We are often encouraged *to pray our experiences*, to become our prayer. If we are tense, we pray our tension and befriend it. If we feel frightened we allow the fear to permeate our prayer and we try to make peace with that fear. It is not the time for wearing masks. We only hurt ourselves in deception. Honesty in prayer reveals projection, prejudice and pride hidden deep inside. This revelation begins the healing. Once we own our emotions and then befriend them, we become aware of a new integrity in our lives. There is more of a swing to our patterns of growth, more of a smoothness and flow to our energy. When the conscious and the subconscious minds interact and resonate with each other in prayer, possibilities for transformation proliferate.

That is why it is so important to acknowledge our feelings when we come to pray which, ideally, would be always. We discern our anxiety, we accept it, we pray it, and we let it go. Likewise with the moment of joy, stress, gratitude, worship. We pray *all* our experiences. We pray our failures, releasing their power when we identify them with the triumph of the failure that ended on the cross. We pray the news—with our daily shock at the human potential for inflicting and enduring pain. We pray these emotions, accepting their truth and making friends with their darkness until all is light. Then we become transparent like God.

Praying our experiences does not come easily. We are challenged to transcend the patterns of our thinking and allow our feelings to color our sharing with God just as we do with our closest friends. Sometimes we need guidance in our search for openness, honesty and integrity when we communicate with the Spirit of love. Luckily there are many sensitively written books and guidelines to facilitate this liberating breakthrough in prayer.

A special word about *the emotion of pain*. It is totally necessary that we befriend and pray our pain. It is a central theme in this book. To live is to suffer. To love is to grieve. Love and pain will always be balanced on the scales of mystery. Praying helps to keep the balance true.

6

Discernible in creation-centered praying will be a movement from "me" to "us" to "you" to service. Personal breakthrough will lead to personal transformation to social transformation. There will be a natural movement toward *action and celebration*.

> In prayer there is sometimes the danger of becoming too wrapped up in oneself, of contemplating one's navel. The concern for "self-improvement" and "self-esteem" may make us inward-looking and self-absorbed, insensitive to the challenge of discipleship in a hungry, frightened and violent world.[12]

In our reflections above on prayer as connecting the energies of our own personal body, the body of our friends and the body of the cosmos, we saw ourselves as recipients and benefactors of life-giving forces. Now we realize that we are empowered in this creative exchange to learn about loving in a new way—to love our bodies, the body of humanity and the body of all non-human creation. In prayer we are sensitive to the accurate assessment and supply of the needs of these bodies. As our slow hearts grow in compassion we make a final commitment in all circumstances and at all times to do the loving thing with justice and in peace. And then we begin to understand and to experience the real meaning of celebration in a new way.

TRUST

The Sleeping Grace

"Why is it that some people do not bear fruit?" asked Meister Eckhart. "Because they have no trust either in God or in themselves. Love cannot distrust." Few find trusting easy. Most people cannot manage it. Yet, without trust, it is as impossible to grow and to "bear fruit" as it is to live without breathing. There is, as Dostoyevsky said, "a temporary surrender of security" every time we risk any kind of positive change. Taking a new step, uttering a new word, is what people fear most. So many are paralyzed even at the thought of a personal risk. The unknown is regarded as the enemy. The universe, for the most part, is not friendly. To trust is to have courage. "Courage," Paul Tillich wrote, "is the daring self-affirmation of one's own being in spite of the powers of non-being."

The ability to trust depends on our childhood experiences. All through childhood there is a constant struggle between the forces of trust and mistrust in the daily encounters of the child: Are my parents trustworthy? Is the world trustworthy? Am I trustworthy?

> One is able to trust because one is confident in oneself, and because of such confidence he can take the risk of conceding complete freedom to the other; if the other rejects me,

then I am still me and worthwhile. Alas, such confidence is not easy to come by, and God protect the poor person whose first attempts at self-disclosure are harshly rejected. Heaven also protect the child who by his very childishness begins life in a situation of trust and finds that trust destroyed by harsh, unloving, manipulating parents who value him not for what he is but for what he can do. Most of those who have impenetrable masks, whose self-defense and self-deception are so pervasive that they do not even realize they are self-defense and self-deception, acquired their masks at their parents' knees. Systematic self-deception, systematic denial which leads to defense mechanisms to protect our shame, is, in the strict sense of the word, neurotic and sick.[13]

The grace of trusting, I believe, is the difference between those who grow and those who do not; between those who have high self-esteem and those who haven't; between those who are creative, imaginative and compassionate and those who are not. Time after time I have searched for the basic difference between people for whom life is usually full and exciting and those for whom it is monotonous and usually dull. Wherein lies the difference? Is it temperament, environment, the presence or absence of personality qualities such as courage, love, knowledge? Or has it to do with trust? Insofar as I can draw on my own experience, the moment of truth came for me when I began to trust in a new way, when I really worked at letting go, and when I made an extra effort to live in the present. These three aspects of a life-approach are intrinsically linked. They are almost interchangeable terms.

When reflecting on the spiritual qualities of our lives—the origin and nature of what are often called graces and virtues—we are again in the land of mystery. If we consider, for instance, the gift of trust, we can identify trust in ourselves, in others, in life itself and in God. Which comes first? And in what se-

quence? The saints and scholars differ in their explanations.
Creation spirituality looks to the basic trust incarnate in creation from the beginning. The moment of the Big Bang (or
whatever in fact set us off on our spinning way) implied a trust
in matter itself. The universe, as Albert Einstein reaffirmed for
us, is friendly and trustworthy. As children of that same universe, we partake in the characteristics of our mother. Without
cosmic trust we die. And cosmic trust, a spirituality of the heart
would have us believe, is the fleshing into time and space, and
ultimately and self-consciously into humanity, the trust that
God is, and, even more amazing, the trust that God has in us.

In *The Transparent Self*, Sidney M. Jourard offers a definition of a psychologically healthy person as one "who displays
the ability to make himself fully known to at least one other
significant human being." For most people this is almost an
impossible challenge. There is a strong tendency to hide from
intimacy, to fear exposure. Deep is the ache to be known and
loved but deep too is the pain of rejection. If one of the greatest
joys is, having revealed oneself, to be accepted and loved, one of
the most hurtful experiences is to be then rejected. That is why
trusting another is tense and risky at the beginning. In the
interests of growing and expanding we make ourselves vulnerable. This is another Christian paradox. To become more, one
must become less. To grow, one must let go. To live more
abundantly, one must be prepared to die. It is still difficult to
believe the extent of God's trust in humanity when he assumed
the weakness and vulnerability of a baby so that people could
one day assume their divinity. Trusting another is dangerous
and exhausting. There is a sense in which we spend ourselves in
believing another. It certainly cost the incarnate God not less
than everything. Nor is there any cheap grace to comfort us in
our attempts at trusting others, ourselves or life itself.

Trusting and sticking by another person means putting our undefended selves on the line in the area of life where we make the best targets. The price is always the same, and it can only be paid by those whose motivation comes from the Spirit. The deepest questions of life, the issues that are of greatest significance to persons, always center on the vulnerability of the human heart in the adventure of love. Hurt is a certainty even in the deepest love; it is as much a part of the pattern of loving as the need to die to ourselves is of the pattern of living.[14]

Psychotherapists and psychologists such as Rollo May and Abraham Maslow have no doubts about the necessity of trust in our lives and about the resistance we offer to the very life-quality that sets us free to grow. This resistance stems from the hurt that loving and trusting brings. We get tired of crying. So we avoid further pain. But there is another reason for our resistance. We are fearful of our own growth. Trusting brings out our finest impulses, our divine creativity. In *Toward a Psychology of Being*, Abraham Maslow writes, "It is precisely the god-like in ourselves that we are ambivalent about, fascinated by, and fearful of, motivated to and defensive against."

A full consideration of our theme calls for some further reflections on trust in ourselves, in others, in life itself and in God. We realize that we are dealing here with a single graceful power which is splintered into many modes and facets in the prism of life-experience. Yet there is but the one elemental energy—the mystery of trust—the mystery which is the backdrop and context for the building of the community of love, the human conspiracy for establishing the divine milieu of justice and peace. What in fact emerges from careful reflection is the truth that without trust the world would end. Without trust we become frozen with fear. There can be no loving if there is no trusting. Nor can there be any living if there is no trusting. Practically everything we do is done in trust, whether it be walking, driving, eating or sleeping. Our hearts stay beating, the world keeps turning, the sun continues to shine.

> The Master would frequently assert that holiness was less a matter of what one *did* than of what one *allowed* to happen.
> To a group of disciples who had difficulty understanding that, he told the following story:
>
>> "There was once a one-legged
>> dragon who said to the centipede,
>> 'How do you manage all those legs?
>> It is all I can do to manage one.'
>> 'To tell you the truth,' said the centipede,
>> 'I do not manage them at all.' "[15]

This reflection is to encourage faltering hearts to take a tiny step outside, to test the ground, to feel the difference, to sense the welcome. This tiny step is, in fact, a "giant stride of soul," the triumph of light over darkness and of love over fear. Each of us needs to repair our damaged sense of trust in the love that underpins all of life, in the possibility of transcendence, in the predictability of the future. "If you trust yourself to the river of life," Krishnamurti promises, "the river of life has an astonishing way of taking care of you." This reflection is to reawaken and rebuild a wounded childhood trust so that we can let go of irrational attachments to past and present securities, of a relentless fear and suspicion of the unknown. The future is a loving mother waiting for us with outstretched arms; the future belongs to an all-powerful being who is crazy about our freedom and our fulfillment and longs only that we abandon ourselves to her care. We act local, we think global and we trust cosmic.

"What God does first and best and most is to trust his

people with their moment in history. He trusts them to do what must be done for the sake of the whole community."[16] I conclude this reflection with reference to the ultimate paradigm of trust, the primordial sacrament of risk and vulnerability, when the all-powerful creator and everlasting lover of all that ever was, is or will be, assumed the precarious fragility of a baby. Because this mystery of incarnation offends the sensibilities of many believers who prefer to obey an indestructible God of judgment, there are many strategies for avoiding the shocking implications of this unique moment. God has entrusted the future of the world into our keeping. We are responsible for expanding the circle of love that heals and saves. We are made accountable for the spreading of the network of trust that will encounter and transcend the fearful forces that war against the bodies and body of love.

Faith, according to Erik Erikson, is the religious expression of basic trust. Something, however, has happened to the concept and the term "faith," at least within Christianity. The meaning of "faith" has strayed, over the centuries, from the notion of belief in a person and of trust in the human heart of Jesus Christ. No longer directly anchored in its original experience of trust, "faith" has devolved into a thing—it has been "reified"—a possession that people have, or have lost, or never had. It is often understood as the capacity to give intellectual assent to set teachings and doctrines drawn up by those in power. For some, the translation of the phrase "faith in God" to "trust in love" comes as a liberating revelation that enriches the commitment of the believer; for others it is meaningless. What has happened is that a certain kind of emphasis on the external practices of religion has led to an almost total eclipse of the underlying reality of trust.

A legalistic understanding of redemption, for instance, has led to a legalistic explanation of the sacraments, investing them with little short of magical powers. To a sacramentally confused believer, baptism becomes the absolutely necessary ritual for the salvation of each individual soul, and going to confession in itself ensured the forgiveness of sins. What was required by law was carried out, and God kept his side of the bargain. It was "earned" grace. There was, therefore, no room for trust in God. The fact that it is always, only, and completely because of God's extravagant mercy that we are accepted and forgiven had become a forgotten truth.

There is a sweet freedom for the soul that recognizes its potential, readiness and need for this insight—when the sleeping grace of trust is awakened and loved into vibrant life. Creation spirituality brings a timely reminder of this basic revelation—that all is gift; we can only *trust* that we are forgiven, loved, saved. This trust is itself a divine gift. All is grace. Profound changes begin to happen once we make this radical paradigm shift in our perception of sacramental celebration. The whole quality of our spirituality is likely to be transformed. An immense amount of letting go begins to happen, especially the letting go of guilt, doubt and their inevitable consequence—the tendency to judge, criticize and condemn others. Above all, the soul breathes again, liberated now from the fearful shadows thrown by past sins and future judgments—shadows that stifle and eventually kill the small spark of divine life precariously flickering deep within. And so the grace of living in the "now" becomes a reality, and the deep peace and joy of the promised abundant life are experienced by the soul grown tired and weary of a faith gone dry for want of life-giving waters of basic trust:

> *Lord, fill me with hope*
> *as a child*
> *that wakes up every morning with*
> *a new look*
> *in her eyes.*

SUMMARY

Growing in Self-Esteem

1. Meditation

We meditate on the wonder and beauty that we are (cf. First Window Summary: Preparing for High Self-Esteem). We are mystics who try to listen to our hearts. We try to bring our hearts to a condition of stillness so that we can see the face of divine love shining within them. Centering and synergism help us to achieve this by drawing from three sources: the energies within oneself, the energies of the universe and the love of one's friends. This kind of connectedness results in an awareness of *power*. We learn how to channel such power so as to put ourselves in control of our lives, to be fearful victims no longer, to free ourselves by getting unstuck from our escapist addictions. Meditating on and visualizing the state of balance leads to the experience of new graces—of lightness, flexibility, resilience and readiness.

2. Acceptance

We accept the way things are, the sub-personalities, the sub-selves that make up our personalities—the child, the teen-ager, the female, etc. We develop a realistic attitude to what is going on. Life is not perfect; neither are those around us. There

are such happenings as necessary losses. I cannot change the
world. I cannot change anything except myself. I can change my
reaction to what happens to me. Nobody can make me feel
inferior without my consent! It takes patience and perseverance
to realize the difference between the event and my response:
over the first I have no control, but my response is my decision.

3. Trust

We trust in God's unconditional love. "Go your way.
Your trust has saved you." Our strange difficulty in, and even
resistance to, believing this stems from our woundedness. We
must trust our heart and our creative powers. This is not to be
confused with lack of decision-making. A sense of responsibility and accountability is central to true self-esteem. But the
central place of trust is beyond question.

4. Mourning

Because we so often deny the grief deep within us, a grief
that arises from our many losses and unfulfilled needs, we are in
dire need of mourning. Until we mourn we cannot be free. This
is especially true for men, because many men know not how to
mourn or what to mourn for. And blame is destructive.

There is a current need for rituals of grief and loss to facilitate movement through the stages of grieving. This is a fruitful
time for growing. Denial is dangerous because of the later emotional distortion it causes. In the absence of public and private
mourning both soul and body become ill. How do we prepare
for the necessary losses?

5. Art-as-Meditation

This description comes from the creation spirituality tradition of extrovert meditation. It refers to the calling forth of the

creative spirit in each one, through the medium of activities carried out in a prayerful manner. The spirit and body are seen as a unity and stimulated into their innate artistry through the imagination. There is no competition or comparing in the reflective painting, clay-work, movement, writing, massage, etc. that is often referred to as art-as-meditation. The heart and mind and body unite and rejoice in creativity and healing.

6. Affirmations

Affirmations empower one to change long-held viewpoints, to deflect the control of others. This conversion is often a silent happening. Here are some examples of affirmations that have facilitated self-esteem and increased confidence. The Christian will pray these in light of the Spirit in whom we live and move and have our being.

"There is no loss which cannot lead to gain."

"If you dare to love, be prepared to grieve."

"We cannot love anything without becoming vulnerable to loss."

"We can only really know and love as much of ourselves as we are willing to share or give away to another."

"Your security is your ability to connect with the cosmic power that creates all things."

"Every cell within your body responds to every single thought you think and every word you speak."

"Every day I recover my power because I can do all things in him who makes me strong."

7. Self-Disclosure and Co-Counseling

We have a deep resistance to the revealing of our deep secrets to another. When I began to do this some years ago, a new self-acceptance and self-esteem started to grow. The art of creative listening has the same effect when the listener is disciplined and sensitive and knows the principles involved. *Dreamwork* will reveal the urgent messages for growth, guidance and creativity that emanate from our deepest and divine selves.

The importance of discovering or creating support groups is central. Without these, growth in self-esteem is very difficult. Without role models also, such growth is very slow and unsure. Growth may be facilitated by partial models, that is, where no one person is adequate to the challenge.

8. Befriend Your Pain

How do we love our wounds, celebrate our scars? By letting the pain be pain. Suffering holds the secret of our growth and joy. In pain there is a readiness, a receptivity, a waiting. Notice the paradox, where the experience of weakness, silence, darkness, emptiness is regarded by the mystic as the womb of creativity. We need to accept the parts of us that we have rejected—to love the enemy within.

Even before the befriending of pain, there is first the readiness to accept the inevitability of it. In current presentations of self-esteem, the avoidance of, or the awkwardness with, this topic is disturbing. What is needed urgently if the movement is to continue is a psychology of pain, *a spirituality of suffering.* Christianity has a familiar theology of the cross to refer to.

9. Living in the Now

Living consciously is another way of talking about "living in the now." It is the grace of noticing, of attentiveness to the present moment, and an awareness of the richness of what is happening. Healing and wholeness spring from this. No masks are worn. The point of power is in the present moment. Each moment we decide our future by our choice of thoughts. At-

tending to the present is the work of the saint; the present is the
only place to live and be. It is the miracle of the ordinary, the
end of dualism. The present moment has within it all that we
need to grow. The present moment is never intolerable.

10. Forgiveness

There is power and affirmation in forgiveness: of each
other, of oneself. Even grace cannot penetrate the hardened
heart. "Heaven is on earth in human forgiveness." Human forgiveness is divine forgiveness incarnate. Reconciliation celebrates this. The Greek word for forgiveness is "letting go"—
letting go of hurt. It is a process of healing. It is the grace of
moving on: the grace of not wanting to punish the one who
hurt us with the very pain that we endured. Forgiveness is the
taking of a positive step toward wholeness in yourself and in the
other. It is the grace to reclaim our power, to stop being a victim
forever because we have been hurt. Our self-esteem cannot live
with the destructive blaming and resentment, or with the resulting addictions to distract us from that open wound. Forgiveness is the letting go that heals the bleeding sore, bringing
inner peace.

11. Healing of Memories

Great damage is done by pushed down, buried-alive childhood hurts and later injustices, and the pain must be acknowledged; it must come out. This is alarming but good. It cannot be
forgotten. The psyche remembers. We bring the pain to the
passion of Christ. There it is redeemed and a new energy is
born. "By his wounds your wounds are healed" (Is 53).

12. The Unconditional Love of God

People with low self-esteem tend to suffer from false
images of God and associated negative feelings and attitudes.

This arises from faulty teachings about God in the first place. It is liberating and healing to contemplate the unconditional love of God (Eph 3:18). Without trust in unconditional love our self-esteem will continue to struggle and grow weak.

13. *Readiness To Let Go*

The heart itself knows the right time. You cannot force the river. For *you*, perhaps the metanoia begins *now*. But in the meantime, letting go is one of the few activities that can be practiced anyplace, at any age, at every moment, even when the light is gone: "In the desert of the heart, let the healing fountain start." Once the movement begins, it continues to roll. The *chakras* are cleaning up and we are taken over by a most loving power. This power does it all. Our contribution is to allow the transformation to take place. We trust, we let go and we live in the now. It is only in the now that the love of life and the pain of life create beauty.

14. *Co-Creators with God*

Picture the image of God as giving birth each day—being green, pregnant, surprising and new. Only through us can this truly happen. We are the builders of the kingdom. We are divine royalty. Our understanding of the humanity of Christ makes us sensitive to the mystery that we each are. Cultivate the desire to create something new and beautiful each day—by, for instance, introducing your friends to each other; by a new way of cooking another meal; by a new sentence, etc. This sense of uniqueness, of the fact that I am absolutely unique in doing things *my* way is basic to self-esteem.

15. *The Artist Within*

We nurture our talent, our creative gifts by being non-judgmental, non-competitive. Eric Gill said that every artist may not be a special kind of person, but every person is a special kind of artist. Rollo May warned that "if you do not express your own original ideas, if you do not listen to your own heart, you will have betrayed yourself." This applies to all we do. As well as the art-as-meditation experiences, one can ritualize the ordinary experiences, e.g. cutting the orange, baking the cake, sweeping the ashes, cleaving the wood, telling a story. This habit of the heart consecrates the ordinary.

In *All I Need To Know I Learned in Kindergarten* Robert Fulghum describes his time in the laundromat as a "religious experience." In the polarities of hot and cold, wet and dry, dirty and clean, he identified the four great elements of air, water, fire and earth. Round and round go the clothes and in his imagination there is the elemental circle, the beginning and the end, the Alpha and the Omega. And for one elegant moment, life has meaning.

16. Resistance

Resistance is a strange power. It is the refusal to change, to grow, to be healed, a great fear of deeper revelation. Even dreams can be kept unremembered because they can be threatening to the status quo of our lives. There are different names for this reality: psychological explanations about the shadow and the love of the inner darkness, and theological ones about original sin and grace.

The *risk* is perceived as very daunting. We have need for beauty but we fear being destroyed by it. Someone said, "Do not be afraid to get to know yourself no matter how beautiful you are." It is in our own creative beauty that we most resemble God. "God is beauty," wrote Irenaeus. "Beauty is eternity here below," said Simone Weil. Gandhi used to say, "Real beauty is my aim." There is no denying the risk and the need for courage. This is a magnificent gift of the Holy Spirit.

Courage is at the heart of the matter here: to look fear in the face and to keep walking, to ask the question that might destroy a relationship in the interests of truth.

17. *The Ministry of Presence*

We have a call to be a comforter. "Counsel" is a gift of the Holy Spirit—to walk alongside, to console the anxious, to calm the confused. We are all called to exercise our healing power. Some are especially called to reflect God's own compassion. Some have a gift for bringing peace and freedom to tormented minds: "Praise be to the Father of compassion and the God of all comfort who comforts us in all our troubles so that we can comfort those in any trouble with the comfort we ourselves have received from God" (2 Cor 3:4). Your heart will tell you if it feels called to be trained in how to listen to and comfort other troubled hearts.

18. *Personal Integrity*

Dishonesty is one of the most potent destroyers of self-respect. Without truthfulness no strategy will work. Do I act hypocritically? Do I behave in accordance with my beliefs and principles? This is a relentless discipline, one which is rarely mentioned in the self-esteem handbooks. There can be no self-esteem without habits of discipline. The lies of life will wage perennial battles to protect their kingdom of darkness. Only the purified light of truth will transform.

Fourth Window

The Wonder of Change

COMPASSION

The Heart of a Woman

The aim of this reflection is to recover the word "compassion" from the shadows and bring it center stage once again. It is a word with profound meaning—a word that gathers in so much of what the *via transformativa* is about. I tend to think of compassion as a feminine virtue, one that is natural to the heart of a woman, one that is uniquely begotten by God our mother. Compassion has a ring of solidarity to it. Because all of us are aspects and images of the one divine source, the appropriate human response to other creatures is one of loving sensitivity. When we forget this elemental fact of our existence, the bond of harmony and peace is broken. This was explained to us with deep feeling one afternoon in May 1988, on a hillside in Oakland, California, by the grandson of Mahatma Gandhi. He was tracing our hunger for peace back to our common origins in God. This concern is cosmic—it is more than the quest for personal healing. Both as individuals and as a planet we are genetically coded for compassion, for "karuna." "Why do men fight?" he asked. Because compassion is dead. "All wars take root," he added, "in the 'I am here and you are there' attitude."

On the day he died, Thomas Merton said,

> The whole idea of compassion is based on a keen awareness
> of the interdependence of all these living beings, which are
> all part of one another and all involved in one another.

That is why compassion is to be distinguished from the kind of pity that makes distinctions—as much pity does—and the kind of love that is sentimental, where one person has a false kind of empathy. The "karunka"—the compassionate person—feels about everybody and everything as she does about her very self. In fact she daily becomes more aware of all creation as herself. When she says "I love you" she is no longer talking about giving or receiving; she means something like "You are that part of me without which I would be less than complete." To be present to life in this way calls for hard-won self-forgetfulness and endless letting-go. This spirituality is not for all. Most of us are only beginning the long journey toward this understanding and vision. St. John of the Cross preached about becoming nothing so that the "all" might be achieved. This kind of talk frightens most of us. It is really scary to step out into the darkness alone, defenseless. Anthony de Mello was aware of this real panic in his listeners' hearts: "When people hear me speak about these things they say, 'Tony, listening to you, one is left with nothing to hang on to . . .' I then complete their sentence: '. . . as the bird said when it began to fly.' "

An awareness of shared weakness is the beginning of compassion. This is its strength. And this is the source of the call. The call is to action, arising from the breaking down of the boundaries between the self and everything else. In the weakness, therefore, is the strength. At a certain time in our lives, our wounds will empower us with vision and with unfamiliar strategies for transformation. We are sensitized to others at the point of our own pain. The tree of our energy grows in the open wound. This healing energy is holistic—it works from the center. And because we know ourselves to be one with the universe, we experience our own healing in the healing of the world. Mother earth heals us. To be compassionate is to be a wounded healer. We redeem and are redeemed even as we breathe. In owning their own suffering, our hearts participate in the cosmic pain of created being. We shine more brightly even as we lose ourselves in the wider wounds of a fallen world. It is not only in the context of suffering that compassion is appropriate. It is about "feeling with" across the range of emotions, and "reaching into" across all barriers. The graces of compassion, for instance, arise from the awareness of our intimacy with the basic rhythms of the first creation. No other word catches this cosmic content, no other word reaches into the common ground of our origins and destiny, no other word expresses the emotional attitude that follows on our recognition of our lineage and extended family. Unlike most other positive emotions to which some element of limit might be placed, compassion, by nature and definition, has no boundaries.

> . . . compassion is about energy we give and take from all creatures, not just from human beings. After all, Martin Buber explained that I-Thou is not only an experience between people but among people and trees, people and animals, people and music and painting and other arts, and people and God. The selling of psychological personalism has often ignored compassion and reduced it to ego-feeling alone, just as it often tends to ignore the mystery and riches of silence and solitude where so much compassion is learned and developed.[1]

A shallow grasp of the infinite depths of the human spirit and its roots in divine love can be quite detrimental to the acquisition of true self-esteem or healthy psychological liberation. I have yet, for instance, to find the word "compassion" mentioned at tutorials or in course descriptions. At this point in our reflections at the windows of wonder, we have moved away from forced and limited interpretations of "self" and "self-esteem." We are moving, in fact, toward a gradual reinterpretation of self, leading to a loss of the dominant self, so that we can become more effective co-creators with God, participating ever more intensely in his life. Our compassion, in fact, may be extended toward God himself. Because God is compassionate, he suffers with the anawim, the poor.

> Human compassion then becomes the relief of the pain of God as well as the relief of human pain. This theme of God in pain is an ancient one, well developed in Judaism and in certain thinkers. . . . Rabbi Heschel, in an interview given a few days before his death, declared, "There is an old idea in Judaism that God suffers when people suffer. There's a very famous text saying that even when a criminal is hanged on the gallows, God cries. God identifies with the misery of people. I can help God by reducing human suffering, human anguish and human misery."[2]

Compassion is about a passion for justice, freedom and peace. This passion is held with the urgency of a mother's commitment to her child. Compassion is powered by the memory of a grounding in a common life-source, by the awareness of the one sacred womb where all life was birthed, by a sensitivity to the unity and connectedness of all creation as though the whole cosmos were one vibrant body. How can I be unconcerned when part of me is oppressed, exploited, manipulated? How can I be unmoved when part of me is ecstatic? These are the questions of the compassionate person, the one who has transcended the self. The self that dies is the self that separates. "I live now, no not I: Christ lives in me," wrote St. Paul. To St. Catherine of Siena the Lord said, "I am he who is; you are she who is not." Anthony de Mello points out that this spirituality named compassion is in tune with the best tradition of Christian mysticism, Muslim Sufism, Hindu Advaita, Zen's atomism and Tao's emptiness.[3] Compassion is pure when it makes no distinction between the "objects" of its loving concern. There is no question of loving others more than myself or of loving God more than others, because there is only being.

For the entire insight upon which compassion is based is that the other is *not* other; and that I am *not* I. In other words, in loving others I am loving myself and indeed involved in my own best and biggest and fullest self-interest. It is my pleasure to be involved in the relief of the pain of others, a pain which is also my pain and is also God's pain.[4]

Before bringing this reflection to an end it is important to consider the necessity of celebration in the flow of compassion. Both compassion and celebration bear witness to the transcendence of self toward "the other," toward cosmos, toward God. Both are set in a social, universal and divine context; neither of them can happen alone.

They are appropriate partners also in their common underpinning of joy. Because the focus of compassion is the fundamental unity of all creation, it touches too on the humor and joy at the heart of all being. One can only celebrate this discovery, the discovery that certain people are reaching the underground river where all the streams unite and the sound they make is the sound of laughter. Because of the wonder of this, and of the sentiments of praise that rise, unbidden, from the heart—dimensions of the *via positiva* of creation spirituality— we reach for the simple and rich symbols of the earth to both interiorize and externalize these glimpses of mystery.

Since worship without sacrifice, according to Gandhi, is one of the deadly sins, the celebration that follows on compassion will carry the clear prints of the *via negativa* in the letting go and detachment that the compassionate person is engaged in. All clinging, distracting attachments, doubting, competing and whatever tends toward dualism must be let go of if the spirituality named compassion is to grow. There is a sense in which we must lose the desire to control and manipulate life in general and our own in particular if our compassion is to stay sensitive and healthy, and if we wish to truly celebrate and not just go through the motions. Matthew Fox is convinced of the intrinsic bond between compassion and celebration. To be compassionate one must forget many things. And this is where celebration is so appropriate.

> For all celebration is an act of forgetting in order to remember. Thus celebration requires acts of forgetting and it is in the very energy expressed in celebrating (for example in folk dancing) that such forgetting and remembering is effected. In celebration we forget the superficial in order to remember the deep. But the deep is simple and good; it invites us to celebrate.[5]

There is a *via creativa* identifiable in the "work of compassion" and in the celebration of that work. One must be free to follow the path of creativity. Only then is one ready to celebrate compassion. The *via negativa* is about liberation. To let go of competitiveness, to transcend self-consciousness, to forget about crippling control, to forgive ourselves radically—these are the ways we become free to be creatively compassionate and to celebrate deeply. In *Circles of Love*, Henri Nouwen writes,

> I am constantly struck by the fact that those who are most detached from life, those who have learned through living that there is nothing and nobody in this life to cling to, are the really creative people. They are free to move constantly away from the familiar, safe places and can keep moving forward to new, unexplored areas of life.[6]

Finally, in creation spirituality the *via transformativa* is about the new creation of a global civilization where justice and peace pervade the community. It is along this path that compassion runs, because the social change envisioned by the mystics and prophets demands, first and foremost, the liberation of the great variety of oppressed creatures, human and non-human, that we daily encounter. To be compassionate is the radical human condition for recognizing, healing and freeing the anawim, a term that includes all victims of blind carelessness and unbridled greed among whom mother earth is becoming daily more noticeable. Readers may remember the lists of spiritual and corporal works of mercy that we learned by heart from the catechisms of yesterday. These lists were a central dimension of compassion-in-action, which is about *creating* community, *making* peace and *doing* justice.

There is a place here for some kind of ritual in this spiritual evolution to hold the network of energies together, a liturgy to gather our past story into the present moment with hope for the future, symbols to express and deepen our compassion and creativity as we grow. One day soon the world will celebrate.

ANAWIM

The Reluctant Prophets

In the Third Window we reflected on one aspect of the mystery of the incarnation and on the way that God is unpredictable in his presences everywhere, surprising us with joy, making us wonder continually at the hidden beauty of all things. Revelation happens in the most unlikely places. It is happening all around us. Gerard Manley Hopkins writes about the just man who

> . . . acts in God's eyes what in God's eye he is—
> Christ—for Christ plays in ten thousand places,
> Lovely in limbs, and lovely in eyes not his
> To the Father through the features of men's faces.

The "loveliness" referred to here is not necessarily of the conventional kind. In this reflection I wish to explore more fully the submerged loveliness of a whole minority section of society —the underprivileged, the rejected, the unheard or the misunderstood or the voiceless—those I call the anawim. The word anawim is a biblical term for those who are oppressed and exploited, who are poor and marginalized, who are unaccepted because they are "different." Creation spirituality holds that such people are very special revelations of God, living paradoxes of his unconditional love and great beauty. They are signs of contradiction in that their very woundedness reveals some special attributes and characteristics about God and about the "abundant life" promised to us here. Toward the end of *The Clowns of God* there is a poignant scene where God speaks to some anxious, well-intentioned people about a mentally handicapped girl in their midst.

> I know what you are thinking. You need a sign. What better one could I give you than to make this little one whole and new? I could do it; but I will not. I gave this mite a gift I denied to all of you—eternal innocence. To you she looks imperfect, but to me she is flawless, like the bud that dies unopened or the fledgling that falls from the nest. . . . She will never destroy. . . . She will remind you every day that I am who I am, that my ways are not yours, and that the smallest dust-mote whirled in darkest space does not fall out of my hand. I have chosen you. You have not chosen me. This little one is my sign to you. Treasure her.[7]

Of the vast array of anawim in every part of the world, I have the mentally handicapped in mind in this section, and in particular I wish to write about Joseph, my forty-six year old brother, who suffers from the Down's syndrome condition and is also a diabetic. I chose the anawim in general (and Joseph as their representative) for this Fourth Window of Change—the *via transformativa*—because of the forgotten quality of what I would term their creation spirituality and its potential for transforming society when the time comes for the world to recognize these reluctant and unlikely prophets of our time. (And yet, while they themselves remain unaware of their prophetic role in the shaping of the future, those of us who are privileged to be part of their lives cannot help but be impressed by the simplicity and elegance of their natural self-esteem.)

When I wonder about Joseph and reflect on the mystery that he is, I often recall the above words of Morris West. I believe that people like Joseph carry a mission to change us, to shock us into growing. The familiar can be a prison. The well-worn path can be a grave. The mystics talk about the need for conversion of heart before we can see clearly, to learn from what is different if we are to be ready for wonder and for sharing in wisdom. People's fear of the handicapped can often be traced to a sinister resistance to what is not "normal." Joseph and his friends challenge us to rethink our conclusions about God. Maybe he is not a western, white, "normal" male! Maybe there is something our divine parent is trying to tell us about love and beauty and the divine self! Maybe we have been assuming too much about right and wrong, about sin and grace, about what is "normal," and especially about God.

People like Joseph are powerful revelations of this perennial truth which we forget at our peril. God is different and always will be. In his own time and in his own way he will gradually reveal the beauty that love is. This I believe he is doing, in a mysterious fashion, in the phenomenon of handicapped human beings. That is why we must not try to change them, but to understand them. Like Jesus himself, but not as clearly, they are windows of God's wonder. If we allow our hearts to be touched by the anawim, we become sharers of divine mystery; deep calls to deep, and our own buried beauty, creativity and compassion awaken. What a truly amazing artist God is who, disguised in the hearts of the anawim, reaches into our fragile hearts, unlocking the prisons of fear where we would otherwise surely die.

The encounter with the anawim is not always straightforward. Handicapped people, for instance, often provoke a kind of anger and fear in us. In our sharing with them, they invite us to look inside ourselves, and then we fear a disturbing discovery. They bring us to a realization of our own illness.

They see through a facade of smiles and friendly words and sense the resentful heart before we ourselves notice it. Often they are capable of unmasking our impatience, irritation, jealousy, and lack of interest, thus making us honest with ourselves. For them, what really counts is a true relationship, a real friendship, a faithful presence. Many mentally handicapped people experience themselves as a disappointment to their parents, a burden for their families, a nuisance to their friends. To believe that anyone really cares and really loves them is difficult. Their hearts register with extreme sensitivity what is real care and what is false, what is true affection and what is empty words. Thus they often reveal to us our own hypocrisies and invite us always to greater sensitivity and purer love.[8]

When we touch on our own woundedness we have to be prepared to bleed for a long time. But in the company of the handicapped, while it may be slow, we will be graced with a sure and radical healing. Jean Vanier reflects:

> In some way their anguish awakened my own anguish, their poverty my own poverty. This is an incredible discovery . . . that the Good News is announced to the poor, not to those who serve them. Our acceptance of handicapped people as they are, with all their disabilities, weaknesses and frailties, teaches us to accept every human being, and ourselves, to accept the fundamental wound inside. . . .

To do this requires a strong heart for a long journey, lots of angels to show the way, trusty companions who laugh a lot, the sun and wind in the right direction, and extra helpings of bread and wine.

Even though he is now slowing down because of damaged kidneys, Joseph is very much alive. He lives on the top edge of his life. Each waking moment he is to be found at the thrusting, raw and urgent verge of consciousness. Since he never went to conventional school, where one's potential is often underestimated, he is forever challenging limitations and forcing boundaries and presuppositions. Conformity is alien to Joseph. He simply does not know its meaning. Like poets, prophets and mystics, he is a menace on the assembly line. Nor is he a supporter of social expectations. To live with Joseph you must loosen up, lighten up and let go of all pretensions to grandeur. He wasn't in the line when they were giving out self-consciousness. He is impervious to class. Everyone is equal. His assessment of what deserves his attention is based on different criteria. At home as he is with bishops, the sight of a crying baby, a bandaged head or any sign of human distress will brook no competition in commanding his full and loving concentration. How strange it is that, handicapped and imprisoned as we often see him to be, he is still the living example of what we might call a free spirit. Nobody taught Joseph to dance.

Many people, they say, die with their music still in them, their songs still unsung, their stories untold. This will never be said of Joseph. His heart is on his sleeve for all to see. Nobody is in any doubt about his preferences. To indicate something of his pure transparency, I will take three examples from his attitude to time, to possessions and to priorities.

Regarding time, one can learn a great deal from Joseph and those like him. His time is sacred time—sacred time for play. While helping him to shave, for instance, each morning of my visits home, when speed is often essential because of bus-time and workshop-time deadlines, he never misses an opportunity to snatch quick kisses between razor strokes, to suggest a brief, rather rough spot of wrestling on the bed before the call of duty, or to initiate a spirited interlude of hide-and-seek even at a moment of domestic tension! To walk with Joseph you must change your pace, your direction and your expectations. You will slow down when you wanted to hurry, hurry when you wanted to stop. You will discover a new timing, new reasons to celebrate, and a strange glimpse of a previously unsuspected joy in living.

Regarding possessions, Joseph travels light: just sufficient for the moment. The storing of material things, the saving of anything inedible, the building of the nest egg for a rainy day— all these attitudes are alien to the special people. The more we have, the more we worry. Not hoarding or clinging sets them free. How can you hug someone, for instance, if your arms are full of things. They seem to have trouble with the concept of ownership, especially when applied to others. There is a story about the Galway woman who was on a shopping spree one hot July afternoon. Overdressed and overspending she was perspiring and frustrated in the crowded store. To calm her nerves she rushed to buy a cup of tea and a packet of biscuits just before the cafe closed. She then plowed her way to a small table in the corner only to find, when she arrived there, that a Down's syndrome man was already seated there. Making no effort to hide her exasperation at this turn of events, she placed her heavy parcels around her, removed her overcoat, and finally opened the packet of seven biscuits on the table. Each time she took one, her unwelcome companion helped himself also to one. Triumphantly he grabbed the seventh biscuit before she was ready to snatch it; but he then carefully broke it in two and offered to share with her. Not wishing to make a scene, but inwardly raging, she hastily swallowed the piece of biscuit, then reached for her coat and belongings. As she got to her feet, her own packet of seven biscuits, lying hidden in her ample lap, rolled gently on to the floor.

Regarding priorities, there is a powerful instinct, in many of the handicapped people I know, to trust in others. Take Joseph again, for instance. Initially he feared the water. Yet, with the affirmation and encouragement of those he trusted, he made the commitment. His inner terror, as I held him in the pool, was matched by his faith in those around him as he joined his equally adventurous companions in the water. And the water, full of love for them, swept under and up around them, supporting them with special care. Like many of his friends, Joseph gives a deeper meaning to the power of trust. He seems to live without a "why" as Meister Eckhart, the thirteenth century mystic and famous supporter of creation spirituality, recommended to all followers of Christ. The majority of the anawim are abandoned to the predictability of love, to the certainty that God will keep his promises. Unlike many of us, and in spite of a variety of deep afflictions, they have no problems in living with unconditional love; in fact, to my mind, this is the only kind of loving that people like Joseph are familiar with. It is their unique identification with God's unconditional love that marks out so many handicapped people as special incarnations among us. And just as not everyone was able to spot the glory in love's first becoming flesh in Jesus Christ, not everyone now finds it easy either.

One gradually becomes aware of many more qualities, rich and precious, in the daily lives of handicapped people. It isn't so much that Joseph is always forgiving. He is not *conscious* of repeated acts of forgiveness—he simply lives a forgiving kind of life. He forgives as he breathes. Blaming, criticizing and holding grudges are rare enough in the lives of many of the anawim. They have some innate suspicion that such a way of life is deeply self-destructive. They love making peace. It is clear and refreshing and a joy to see, when, still crying from sheer physical hurting, Joseph never fails to embrace the doctors and nurses at the hospital, who have spent his checkup day sticking necessary needles into his arms, paring his corns untouchable by all but my mother, or applying medicine to the painful piles that bring their own special pain. There is no carry-over of blame. There are stories about the way that God cannot remember our past sins. Apparently the divine lover's memory is highly suspect in this regard! It is a quality of mercy that God shares with people like Joseph. It gives one confidence in the final judgment.

Another arresting quality that can be identified at its most authentic among the ranks of the mentally different is the quality of reverence. It seems to have gone out of fashion these days and the world is the poorer for its passing. But when you watch the way our special friends pick up a baby, accept or offer a present, refuse or agree to an invitation or request, taste a new delicacy or volunteer to meet a new challenge, above all in the manner in which they poke fun at or mimic someone, you will sense what is still called reverence, a sense of respect for something sacred, a delicate awe in the face of human encounter, a sensitivity to the grace-filled moment, a sense of privilege and gratitude at being a participator in life. Their joy seems to lie in being present to, rather than in doing and achieving. (Long before work becomes boring, the likes of Joseph will put down tools!) They have a willingness to see and accept the unfamiliar, to appreciate rather than be threatened by what is different, to be filled with reverence at what we do not even notice.

Anyone living or working with the handicapped will be familiar with their constant urge to celebrate. And there is a consistency and style about their readiness. For most of us, work has become so serious, and guilt, when we take time off from our labors, rides so high, that there is an almost desperate dimension to the way we fling ourselves into our jobs and then into our predictable and routine parties. But the handicapped have an *attitude* of celebration that falls into remission only when they are asleep. Most mornings Joseph wakes up singing for pure joy. The high points of his life have to do with joining happy groups, "Faith and Light" gatherings, weddings and any occasion where music, dancing, singing and lots of people come together. With such celebration, the mystics tell us, we are already creating justice and peace in our midst.

Basically their sense of celebration hinges on the present moment. They are more aware than we are that the present moment is never intolerable. It is the memories from the past that continue to hurt, the fears about the future that relentlessly depress. The present moment is always bearable, livable, potentially healing, and therefore capable of being celebrated with a shindig. It is interesting to reflect on the truth that happiness is not caused by anyone or anything; it is uncaused. We find it difficult to understand that nobody can truly make us joyful in any lasting way. It can only come from the spirit within. It is only our conditioning, our social programming, that prevents us from appreciating their celebratory dimensions of each moment. This characteristic of Down's syndrome women and men is not entirely the same as playfulness or just having a good time. It can also be discerned by a deep-seated love of ritual and ceremony, a very marked sense of the sacred. It is more directly linked with ceremonies such as the official worship of the church. It has to do with sacraments and sacramentals, with processions and devotions. When one observes the total absorption as they participate in good liturgies, they seem to recognize a familiar place, a country they knew before, where they had many friends whom they will meet again, friends who are very supportive, especially at times such as these, during their mission of mercy among us, on this lovely planet earth.

Since I wrote this a few months ago, Joseph died from renal failure. As the evening came on Monday, January 15, 1990, he smiled from his bed of pain at some invisible beauty and, like a flame in the breeze, he swiftly left us.

NOW

My Name Is "I AM"

One of the most beautiful areas in the world is the Puget
Sound region in the Pacific Northwest. Here, a short half-
hour drive north of Seattle, one finds Whidbey Island,
surrounded by the Olympic mountains to the west, the
Cascade range to the east, Mount Baker to the north, and
Mount Rainier to the south.[9]

It was during the ferry ride to the island, entertained by dancing
dolphins, that a deeper understanding and experience of living
in the "now" came to me. This window into the "sacrament of
the present moment" was deepened when we arrived at the
Chinook Learning Community in south Whidbey, a place of
greenness and peace, a spiritual colony of the future. Discovering and repossessing the "now-space" between bitter regret and
anxious foreboding is a liberating and enriching transition. It is
far more than changing one's thoughts or making a mental
effort to concentrate. There is a refocusing on the senses, a
conscious shifting of perception so that a new order of attention
is achieved. By a letting go of deeply distracting and stubbornly
entrenched habits of mind there is a surrender to the flow of
energy as it is happening each passing moment. On that bright
April morning as Kathy and I scanned the green-blue waters for
a glimpse of the orcas, the beautiful killer whales, I became

aware of the movement into the present as a kind of freedom—
almost an escape—from useless confusions and draining specu-
lations. It was like climbing a strong and clear mountain after
wandering for ages in the dark and uncertain underbrush of
shadows, a proud mountain that demanded the full attention of
the climber, yet offered at the same time a perspective on the
climber's life. It is this perspective that is liberating, lifting the
tormented spirit beyond the reach of depression or panic.

> It is certain, this I know, that when we are fully present,
> concentrated, completely involved with what we are doing,
> fear's chilling touch cannot reach us. Here-and-now we are
> perfectly safe.[10]

The present moment is always protective; it is never beyond our
capacity to endure; it is the only place where the pace is right.
Not even hand baggage is allowed when you enter the now, and
the speed restrictions are unique. Any change in pace and one
has moved into the past or the future.

Before the channel-crossing to the village of eco-education
that morning, my mind was alternating between indulgent nos-
talgia and fruitless apprehension. Letting go of my mind and
coming to my senses, allowing the present to flood into me with
its colors and shapes, smells and sensations, expressions and
feelings, was like finding a place of harmony and oneness in a
land of war. It was like existing in another kind of time.

A rather fanciful story illustrates this. Pursued by a hungry
lion a man reached the top of a cliff and, finding a convenient
rope, he slithered halfway down the sheer rockface to where
the rope abruptly ended. Above him a hungry lion was clearly
disappointed and impatient. Below him the turbulent waves
crashed high against the jagged shale. It was a desperate situation. Our human pendulum noticed a shiny, red strawberry

growing with gusto at eye level. Carefully he plucked and sampled it. "This," he said, "must be the tastiest berry I ever ate."

The contemplative life is not a life that distinguishes between the sacred moments and the secular ones in a person's daily life. It is rather a way of living that transforms every moment into a window of wonder through which the invisible world becomes visible. Life in the "now" makes time transparent. When time loses its opaqueness, allowing the real presence of things to impact the human spirit, then every hour becomes God's hour. We steal away into eternity through the gateway of the "now," the unique path of immanence that leads to God's incarnate presence. Incarnation reveals that God's time is now. It was God's will from the beginning to find his fullest expression in time. God cannot be encountered except in the present moment. Anxiety about how love will care for us in the future will get us nowhere. Neither will our concern about how our past history will affect that future.

> I was regretting the past
>   and fearing the future.
> Suddenly my Lord was speaking:
> "My name is I AM"
> He paused.
>   I waited.

>   He continued.
> "When you live in the past
> with its mistakes and regrets,
> it is hard. I am not there.
> My name is not I WAS.

> When you live in the future,
> with its problems and fears,
> it is hard. I am not there.
> My name is not I Will Be.

When you live in this moment
it is not hard. I am here.
My name is I AM."

To perceive love, Krishnamurti reminds us, we must be *present* to it and surrender to it. That is why we have all we need within any one instant. This may sound a little strange. But it is one of the most important truths of creation spirituality. Each instant is the only place of encounter between our spirits and the Spirit of all life, between our emptiness and the universal flow of divine energy. It is here that healing happens. It is here that our creative instincts are awakened, that our likeness to God is revealed and perfected. That is why God created life in time and space in the first place. This we know from the incarnation. God created as he did so that love could empower the universe. Where humanity is concerned, the flow of loving power is often blocked. The combination for unlocking the barriers and restoring the flow is the present moment. That is why we have hope. We can trust what happens because there will never be a time which is not *now*. Love remains constant. "God is always at home," Meister Eckhart used to say; "it is we who go for a walk."

The present moment is where the pen-point of infinite love meets the page of humanity as the divine drama of incarnation unfolds. To read the story, you must stand very close. Living in the now is about the way we are present to what happens. It is about listening with our hearts.

Where shall I look for enlightenment?
Here.
When will it happen?
It is happening right now.
Then why don't I experience it?
Because you do not look.

What should I look for?
    Nothing. Just look.
At what?
    Anything your eyes alight upon.
Must I look in a special kind of way?
    No. The ordinary way will do.
But don't I always look the ordinary way?
    No.
Whyever not?
    Because to look you must be here. You are
    mostly somewhere else.[11]

Another Zen master celebrated his enlightenment by saying: "Oh wondrous marvel: I chop wood, I draw water from the well." There is here a total unification of body, mind and spirit, a complete presence to every sensation. To be devoid of memories and anticipations may seem a rather boring state of mind to endure but it is rich and exciting beyond measure. For the first time in our lives we hear the silent music and behold the hidden masterpiece.

Once, as they rested on a chase, a debate arose among the Fianna-Finn as to what was the finest music in the world.
    "Tell us that," said Fionn, turning to Oisin.
    "The cuckoo calling from the tree that is highest in the hedge," cried his merry son.
    "A good sound," said Fionn. "And you, Oscar," he asked, "What is to your mind the finest of music?"
    "The top of music is the ring of a spear on a shield," cried the stout lad.
    "It is a good sound" said Fionn.
    And the other companions told their delight: the bellow of a stag across the water, the baying of a tuneful pack heard in the distance, the song of a lark, the laughter of a gleeful girl, or the whisper of a frightened love.

"They are good sounds all." said Fionn.

"Tell us, chief," one ventured, "What do you think?"

"The music of what happens," said great Fionn, "that is the finest music in the world."[12]

It is rarely heard, this silent music. And there is no encore. This is the sad part, the cause of much guilt and deep regret, because there is no second chance. In *A Time for Love*, Eugene Kennedy refers to the story in *Our Town* when Emily wants to go back to life for a day.[13] She is warned that as well as living out these happy hours she must watch herself living them, with the knowledge she has of the deaths that happened afterward. She chooses her twelfth birthday. "But it is indeed filled with pain, the pain of seeing how important the everyday meaning of life is and of how little this is realized during the moments we live it." Emily now speaks into the recreated past that cannot hear her. "Oh Mama, just look at me one minute as though you really saw me. Just for a minute now we're all together. Mama, just for a minute we're happy. Let's look at one another. . . . I can't. I can't go on. Oh! Oh! It goes too fast. We don't have time to look at one another. I didn't realize all that was going on and we never noticed." Emily goes back to her grave, overwhelmed by realizing the richness of life that is taken so much for granted during the ordinary living of it. "Oh earth," she says in a fine Christian affirmation of what really counts, "you are too wonderful for anyone to fully realize you. Do any human beings ever realize life while they live it—every, every minute?"

Not many. We are a distracted generation. I have so often feverishly planned ahead. The awaited moments were marred by my anxiety concerning their ending. And when would they come again? In my distractedness I failed to enjoy the special time. How often one sees frantic tourists taking pictures of places they never really were. We are either going toward or coming from without ever truly arriving. We are always either preparing for or restoring after and somehow miss the middle. How different was the boatman's reply to the pilgrims that he ferried across the water to the place of worship. No, he had not been to the shrine because he had not yet taken in all that the river had to offer!   *SEE THE BEAUTY & pain where you are. ARE.*

Is cooking a meal, learning a skill, studying a language always a preparation? Is there not a fullness in every moment no matter what the content or context? There is a story about the explosion of power when someone really concentrates on the immediate detail in the here and now. In the medieval towns of Palestine there were teachers who revealed the mystery of reading and writing to all those who so wished, having at their disposal too the time and the money for such a privilege. These teachers sat at the city walls, using the smooth surface as a "blackboard" whenever necessary. One day a well-dressed Arab approached a teacher and asked to be taught the alphabet. The fee was agreed upon and the teacher, impressed by his stately student, estimated the amount of time required for such a modest goal. He launched into his task with pedagogical flair, but once he had talked about, pronounced and drawn the first letter of the alphabet—aliph—his distinguished pupil asked to withdraw from the class as he wished to concentrate on what he had just learned. The teacher disagreed and argued that even the youngsters could master the whole alphabet in half an hour. Promising to return when he had completed his homework, the mature student departed. Some months later he returned for another lesson. The teacher remembered him and sarcastically requested a demonstration of successful learning. With a sliver of slate the well-dressed man drew the letter "aliph" on the smooth surface. And the wall fell.

To attain such concentration, to become totally present to what is going on, to master the art of living in the "now," a profound level of "letting go" must be reached. The mind is slow to give up its controlling habits. Trusting never comes easily. Remember the man who was chased by the lion and found himself suspended halfway down the cliff face at the end of his rope. "Help me, O God," he shouted. "I have faith in your power." "My son," said the voice from heaven, "I will save you. Only one thing I ask. Let go of the rope." After a long pause the dangling doubter shouted again: "Is there anyone else up there?"

Creation spirituality calls us out of our heads and away from abstractions. The invitation is to come to our senses. Only there is the "now" and only there is the "new." God came to his senses in the incarnation. It was God's wish from the very beginning to redeem and empower us through incarnate present-moment ever-youthful love. "People who dwell in God," Meister Eckhart promises, "dwell in the eternal now. There, people can never grow old. There, everything is present and everything is new."

ONENESS

The Perennial Allurement

Whenever I introduce people from different ends of the planet to each other, I am often struck by the fact that within minutes they have focused in on at least one person they know in common. A little reflection has clarified the situation. *Bottom Line* researchers have established that the vast majority of people in the world are linked by no more than two intermediaries. They have also concluded that two of the most isolated people in the world—say a monk in Tibet and a hermit in Appalachia—are linked by no more than eight intermediaries.[14] Philosopher and scientist Guy Murchie turns poet to communicate his sense of the interrelatedness of everybody.

> *What relation is a white man*
> > *To a black man?*
> *A yellow man to a red or brown?*
> > *Closer maybe than you'd think.*
> *For all family trees meet and merge*
> > *Within fifty generations, more or less—*
> > *In round numbers a thousand years:*
> *Which makes all people cousins,*
> *Siblings in spirit if you will.*
> > *Or, to be genetically precise,*
> > *Within the range of fiftieth cousin.*[15]

Creation spirituality would bid us pursue the phenomenon of oneness still further. The fundamental interconnectedness and perennial allurement of all things for each other belongs to the exciting realms of deep mystery and emerging mysticism. Mysticism is all about interconnectivity. Fritjof Capra is a creation-centered physicist. "The universe," he writes, "is seen as a dynamic web of interrelated events." And the mystic Eckhart points out that "Everything that is in the heavens, on the earth, and under the earth, is penetrated with connectedness, penetrated with relatedness." Having indicated the manner in which humanity's family includes the animal kingdom, the whole of nature including trees and rocks, and the galaxies uncountable, Guy Murchie continues,

> There is no line, you see, between these cousin kingdoms,
>   No real boundary between you and the universe—
>   For all things are related,
> Through identical elements in world and world,
>   Even out to the farthest reaches
>   Of space.[16]

The emergence of a living cosmology is revealing ever-new depths to the mystery of unity. As the physicists explore relentlessly into the dark secrets of space, they confess to continual astonishment at the recurring patterns and harmonic flow that stem from and tend toward a ubiquituous oneness, the reawakening of a vibrant mysticism, from a long sleep, also bringing home to us the interdependence of all living things which are all part of one another and involved in one another. In the creation tradition all people are mystics. The Jewish scholar Abraham Heschel wrote:

> The mystics, knowing that man is involved in a hidden history of the cosmos, endeavor to awake from the drowsi-

ness and apathy and to regain the state of wakefulness for
their enchanted souls.

Gandhi saw all life as one in a cosmic family in which each
member helped to elevate the whole from a selfish, destructive
level to a spiritual and productive one. And not only among the
"major world religions" do we find insights into the mysterious
oneness at the heart of everything but also among the more
ancient and more earth-centered traditions of native peoples all
over the world. "The earth and myself are of one mind," wrote
Chief Joseph of the Nez Perce Indian tribe over one hundred
years ago; "the measure of the land and the measure of our
bodies are the same."[17] Such creation-centered reflections on
"oneness" are sometimes cosmological, sometimes mystical.
These disciplines are intrinsically connected. The mystical experience is like the mirror image of science, a direct perception of
cosmic oneness, an inside window into the mystery that science
grapples with from the outside.

It is easy to maintain the sense of excitement and movement in this vision of intimacy at the heart of all created and
uncreated being. The nature of the primordial oneness is described and imaged in a variety of ways that portray a trusting
dynamism—a flowing, an awakening, a dancing, an allurement,
a loving, a creating, a returning.

> "The world is a spinning die," according to an old Hasidic
> passage, "and all things turn and spin and change, for at the
> root all is one, and salvation inheres in the change and
> return of things."[18]

But the symphony is rarely complete. There are usually
instruments missing or out of tune. Or the acoustics are inadequate. There is often hard wax in the ears, or people's hearts are
distracted. The magic is missed. The whole symphony is less

perfect when the tiniest note is untrue. There is a Pigmy legend about the forest filled with the beautiful music.

> A little boy finds the bird with the enchanting song and brings it home. He asks his father to bring food for the bird. The father refuses to feed a mere bird, so he kills it. And the legend says that with the killing of the bird he kills the song, and with the song, himself. He dropped dead and was dead forever.[19]

Every hurt we cause nature leaves a scar on ourselves. Every time we honor the smallest creature we honor ourselves. Once a Zen master stood up before his students and was about to deliver a sermon. And just as he was about to open his mouth a bird sang. "The sermon," he said, "has been delivered."

I wish to devote the remainder of this consideration of oneness and intimacy to a brief reflection on the unity and ecstasy of sexuality. I will also endeavor to reveal the cosmic and mystical dimension of this unique and precious gift of God. I submit that human sexuality may be regarded as the sacrament of all-loving oneness and healing wholeness. It is the thrust toward unity, the energy within the human being calling for a breakthrough and a breakout from the physical and psychic loneliness that is never far from the human heart. True sexuality-in-action has a multiple unitive power. The persistently reopening wounds at the split between ourselves and the universe are in sore need of healing. In our sexuality we perceive the allurement of union at many levels. In its ecstasy we are in touch with the ecstasy of God. We discover that we are indeed a part of everything and one with the mystery of life. Our sexuality perceived as gift brings home to us our createdness: when perceived as power we are moved by our creativity. "To talk about God in relation to our sexuality," writes Dorothee Soelle, "means to be aware of love moving in us because in God we live and move and have our being." In *To Work and To Love* she writes passionately about the vulnerability involved in true union and about the play of ecstasy and trust in achieving it.

> In long-term relationship, we move between the poles of ecstasy and trust, sometimes closer to one, sometimes closer to the other.... These essential dimensions of our lovemaking are also expressions of our love of God, our relatedness to the source of life. We relate to God in ecstasy and trust....[20]

Creation spirituality reminds us that our creation in God's image means that we are created to become lovers like God, to be allured eternally toward the perfect oneness that God is.

> Sexuality is a sign, a symbol, and a means of our call to communication and communion.... The mystery of our sexuality is the mystery of our need to reach out to embrace others both physically and spiritually. Sexuality thus expresses God's intention that we find our authentic humanness in relationship.[21]

If oneness is the perennial allurement in our lives, fragmentation is always a diminishment. Separation and loss, both cosmic and psychic, in childhood and in maturity, leave heavy shadows on the soul. But we remember the unity from which we came and to which we yearn to return. Sexuality is the guardian of our origins and the guarantee of our fulfillment.

> Relatedness to all that lives is the original experience which we lose in the process of differentiating and creating ourselves as individuals. Lovemaking is an attempt to find our way back to the old unity.... Sexuality reignites in us the oceanic feeling of an indissoluble oneness with the

surrounding world . . . we undo the loss, assuage the grief, and recover a kind of passionate, primitive joy in our exis- tence . . . the time of separation and coldness ends; we enter another time. God is with us; we shall not want.[22]

It will take a long time to restore the mystery of sexuality to where it truly belongs—among the most beautiful windows of wonder onto the love that is God. A fog of suspicion still surrounds this rich and amazing gift of the human expression of love. Rarely within contemporary Christianity is it understood as one of the foremost incarnations of the infinite love that creates, sustains and quickens all life. In fact, along with sin, it is one of the dimensions of human life where we are not encour- aged to search for the experience of the grace of the abundant life. All my memories of past studies of human sexuality have to do with temptations, anxieties and degrees of moral culpability. To recover an understanding of sexuality that gives rise to grati- tude and praise for such freely offered ecstasy, there is a need to revision our theology and spirituality. Sexuality can only be truly celebrated when it is returned to its original roots in cos- mology and mysticism. Personally I have relied on the insights provided by incarnational theology and creation spirituality— insights which have given rise to these reflections—to open up to me a clear new window on to whole expanses of this forgot- ten garden of divine delights.

The Song of Songs in the Hebrew scriptures is one of the finest biblical examples of a cosmic and mystical sexuality. It is cosmic in that the lovers return their love to the universe that gave it birth.

Love is always about a cosmology. Lovers exist in a uni- verse, not just in a personal relationship. Thus, for exam- ple, when the woman responds to her lover's comment on the secret fountain (in the Song of Songs), she includes an incantation to the winds of the universe:

> The fountain in my garden is a spring of running
>   water
> flowing down from Lebanon.
> Arise, north wind!
> O south wind, come!
> Blow upon my garden, let its alluring perfumes pour
>   forth.
> Then will my lover come to his garden
> and enjoy its choice fruits. (4:15–16)

. . . In this poem we are told that the lovers emerged "out of
the wild, up from the desert, leaning and holding." To
make love is to enter the cosmological wilderness, to go
beyond the human artifacts of city and civilization, to return to the depths of darkness where spirit embraces matter and the Cosmic Christ is recognized as earthy and
untamed.[23]

In *Year of the Heart* I have explored these themes more
fully.[24] Human sexuality is healthy and full only when the cosmic connection is made. It is a participation in a wider and
deeper ecological and universal bonding that began with the
primordial act of creation and has evolved into a uniquely beautiful self-conscious exchange of creative love. Cut off from its
cosmic roots and power our love-making will be less holy, our
physical praise less true. "With my body I thee worship," countless couples have solemnly promised at the Christian sacrament
of marriage. Why, I wonder, was this phrase dropped from the
new ritual?

Creation spirituality places human sexuality high on the
short-list of original blessings. It calls for a mystical sexual
awakening. The mystical dimension lies in the ecstasy of unity,
in the playfulness of passion, in the vulnerability of trusting and
in the sacredness of creativity. A comment from C.J. Jung is
appropriate here:

Normal sex life, as a shared experience with apparently similar aims, further strengthens the feeling of unity and identity. The state is described as one of complete harmony, and is extolled as a great happiness ("one heart and one soul")—not without good reason, since the return to that original condition of unconscious oneness is like a return to childhood. . . . It is, in truth, a genuine and incontestable experience of the Divine, whose transcendent force obliterates and consumes everything individual, a real communion with life and the power of fate.[25]

Human sexuality, it seems, is at the heart of the divine, creative power of the universe.

SUMMARY

Spreading Self-Esteem

1. Social Transformation

There is no dichotomy between the personal pursuit of sanctity and the commitment to social transformation. Extreme positions are taken on the debate. But we save our souls even as we save the soul of the world, and vice versa. We pray for a wider sense of responsibility, for an awareness of our oneness with each other and with the earth, and within ourselves. In the healing of ourselves is the healing of the world. The incredible interdependence between our own microcosmic body and the macrocosmic body of the cosmos is daily becoming more significant at a popular level. We put our own creativity at the service of all creation. We are called to be prophets and transformers: to awaken people to the destruction of the human family and to the severely damaged planet we live on.

2. Global Awareness

Millions today are responding to the call to champion the earth in its agony. There is a spreading consciousness of the serious challenge to the environment. This urgency is relentlessly proclaimed by the swiftly increasing thousands of groups around the world, by famous individuals including writers, artists and entertainers, by governments, and by Christian church authorities.

There is a growing outrage at the destruction of the human family and its mother earth. They call to our social responsibility to be concerned about the eroding of topsoil and of the ozone layer, about the polluting of the water and of the air, about the regular annihilation of hundreds of precious and irreplaceable species of flora, fauna and fishes.

3. Institutional Sin

A new balance is emerging between an individualistic approach to personal sin and a responsibility for institutional sins where we perceive the absence of gospel values. What is my attitude to consumerism, militarism, racism, sexism, ageism, the plight of third world countries, elitism, fanatical nationalism (leading to torture and persecution) and the ecological sins of pollution and exploitation of our beautiful and fragile land?

4. Compassion

We each have the capacity for compassion for the "anawim," today's poor. Who are they—the tortured, the oppressed of any regime, the earth's own body? The power of injustice, when it becomes part of the establishment, is almost impossible to dismantle; it tends to become identified with democratic law and order. It takes insight to perceive this, compassion to be shocked by it, and courage to do something about it. How are these forces to be resisted at all costs?

Recent church and papal papers courageously address some urgent contemporary issues such as sexism, violence, ecology and racism. We are being challenged to see all as interdependent. But basically it is the power of compassion that transforms hatred and greed and that builds a kingdom of peace. The *passion for justice* flows from compassion. It stems from a vision of equality and oneness. The joy, sorrow or freedom of another is mine.

Compassion often grows from our wounds; most workers for peace come from dysfunctional homes, likewise with helpers of the handicapped, drug abusers, etc. We are usually aroused most at the point of our pain; our commitment is born in our wounds. Our source of energy is the well of our hurting. It is here that we develop a sense of calling, to become part of the universal flow of compassion. And it all comes back to us; in healing the planet I heal myself; in forgiving myself I forgive all others. In my compassion I am being healed. The beauty of God's compassion, his intense love for the weakest of his family, is incarnated in us.

5. Creative Work

A boring job can slowly destroy me; creative work can redeem and be a power for change. When there is alignment between my deep desires, my abilities and my chosen work, transforming energies are generated. Most people long for such a unity, and many achieve it, sometimes at a great price, by *choosing* their own work. This, of course, is not always possible for any number of reasons, but more and more people seem to be doing it. "Do what you love," the title of Marsha Sinetar's best-seller reads, "the money will follow."

There are four windows to the vision and actualization of freely chosen creative "heart-work." The first window is the conviction that our daily task becomes part of our destiny. The second window is about the insecurity and doubt that mark the movement into a new work environment. Through the third window we visualize the healing service that results from the connectedness and concentrated flow that springs from such a move. (Words like "passion," "sacred" and "devotion" are used by Marsha to describe such vocational involvement.) Finally, life is transformed: it becomes purposeful and exciting. This transformation spreads because such focusing of energy is a compelling and challenging phenomenon.

6. *Justice and Freedom*

The fourth window in the house of creation spirituality offers a perspective on these issues as well as on compassion and celebration. It is the mystery of oneness that holds the healthy tension at the heart of such graces. Compassion, for instance, is about justice-making and is built on the conviction that we are all part of each other's joy and sorrow. To lessen another's pain is to lessen one's own; to heal a little of the pain of the world is to relieve the pain of God. What is needed is a passion for justice and freedom. Through justice of the heart people are loved into transformation. Confrontations and threats only irritate the unjust. Erotic justice is about heartfelt commitment to the search for broken strangers with words and acts of comfort. Only love matters. Only love causes justice. Only love disarms injustice. We are called to trust it.

7. *Signs of Hope*

There is a new awareness, a new consciousness among an increasing number of people. The excitement of the gospel challenge among Christians is generating a conspiracy of earth-saviors. Liturgical cosmic symbols and planetary prayers, new educational programs with emphasis on the artistic in everyone and on right-brain creativity, feminist spirituality, deep ecumenism, the call to our child to celebrate, the return to a creation tradition that is rooted in the gospels—all of these movements are sensitizing countless Christians to exciting responsibilities and possibilities in preparing for the renewal of

the face of the earth. Governments too are at last waking up to
the precariousness of the future.

8. Celebration

Within the Christian community the renewal of liturgical
principles and practice has restored the communal nature of
worship and celebration. There is a corresponding lessening of
a self-centered individualistic kind of attendance at liturgical
functions and "celebrations." The return of passion and play, of
a Celtic spirituality of celebration and justice, will bring an end
to the cynicism and indifference which only lead to despair.
Mechtilde of Magdeburg refers to God as the divine playmate
who brings out the child in us. Ideally, a sense of play would
permeate all our activities and become our permanent attitude
to life. As I write this, I remember the following verses from the
book of Proverbs which were read at this morning's eucharist.
Today is Trinity Sunday.

> *Then was I (Wisdom) beside him as his craftsman*
> *And I was his delight day by day;*
> *Playing before him all the while,*
> *playing on the surface of the earth;*
> *And I found delight in the sons of men.*

9. Worship

All that has been said about celebration and play above
applies to worship, too. There is a kind of seriousness that can
destroy ritual, a self-consciousness that strikes at the roots of
celebration. True worship will allure the wounded child to
come out to play and be healed. There will often be tears. The
pain will be our private story; it will also be the universal suffering of all creation, groaning in this critical moment of its evolu-

tion. It is the crooked shadow of the sin of the world that falls from worship. Hence the old lamentations, the elegant Latin chants of the traditional requiem mass. This is where the pain is drawn into the light, and, through the public mourning, the stages of healing begin.

For worship to be authentic it must be physical. There is still the suspicion of the body, an apprehension about matter. Our rituals, with their healthy ancestry in the universal symbols of water, light, air, bread and wine, were almost "spiritualized" out of existence. So too was a sense of the body in looking, touching, embracing and moving freely. These bodies of ours express the desires of the cosmos to worship its divine life-force; they make it possible for the universe to praise its creator; they are the thanks-giving of all creation; they are the reverence and wonder of the sun, the adoration of the moon and of all the stars, the ecstasy of the wing-folk, the fin-folk and all the four-legged creatures, and the delight of everything that moves and grows.

When a cosmic dimension is once again identified within Christian worship, a powerful agent for universal change will be released. There is an urgent need for the purification and redemption of liturgy at the moment, effective though it is in many places. It must be set free from the tyranny of inappropriate rubrics, for the true celebration of the divine origin, perennial support and ultimate destiny of all creation.

Our worship, dear faithful reader, must be free, as the spirit is free; and it must be for always, as the spirit is for always . . .

> And he to whom worshiping is a window, to open but
>   also to shut,
> has not yet visited the house of his soul whose windows
>   are from dawn to dawn.

A Deep End: Dive of Passage

Four Windows on Water-Wonder

Three things happened to me in the spring of 1989: I learned to swim and dive; I was introduced to, and looked through, the four windows of creation spirituality; I experienced intensely the pain and joy of letting go and growing in my personal life. *Dive of Passage* is my attempt to hold together the magic of those liberating moments.

1. *The Water and the First Window of Wonder*

The day was warm. The sun was near. No worry drifted by. The wavy pool was bright with light. I felt a welcome here I had not felt before. I sensed a love-pull from the water—as though it were a part of me I had forgotten.
No stranger now and unafraid, I knew a wholeness that went
        back
so far my mind began to tremble.
To the time-before-time when gods had splooshed in tuneful
        play
and swam the planets into place,
And ever since that airy time, the power and glory of an older
love is mirrored clear in water.
She incarnates a lovely part of God and so she is
a special kind of sacrament.
Blessed I was, that blue-green day,
Deep blessed and graced I knew myself to be.
A million tiny liquid voices filled my soul with joy so pure.
My startled heart beat out its quiet applause.

A strange exchange it was that happened on that deep-green
        day.
It was the hour of silent telling,

of whispered secrets—deep to deep—across two
chasms-full of mystery.
And yet the news was old, not new. My hungry heart
    acknowledged
what it already knew: in love we were from birth:
we issued forth so many moons ago when God and wisdom
played the planets into being.
And we were dancing still, in spaces new,
to silent tunes that filled the nights of Eden.

How proud I was in this great revelation; how much I loved,
how drawn toward deeper union.
My waiting and my longing now were over. Clear into focus
leaped my faint and hazy readiness
for identifying my pristine love.
For this was I created, this moment was I born.
It was so simple; so easy and so true.
It was the dawning of the seventh day,
a God's-eye view of tumble-flowing creatures
here and there in joy between the nameless oceans.

A kind of trust it was I felt that day,
a kind of trust I ached for in the past but never knew.
I trusted now, that at the fractured point of pain
the healing soon would happen.
My heart would then begin
to love her wounds, embrace the flaws.
Oh, there was mercy in the water; the promise of a midnight
greening with the proud goddess of blessing.
And there would be a journey where the past and future
spoke a present tense and where, ahead,
her lovely limbs all wet and shiny,
the wild and timeless child of promise
would water-dance us home.

2. *The Dive and the Second Window of Darkness*

It is so lonely here: so high, so insecure.
The icy fingers of familiar fear are chilling now,
around my heart—as usual.
So much to lose . . .
O God, so much to lose.
At this grey hour the water hard below reflects the brittle
sun above. The board beneath my feet began to tremble.
"You cannot win"; each hollow echo fills my soul and mocks
     me
while I climb the fourteen station-steps
along the hill of thin decision.
It is so cold and quiet:
there is a deadly silence:
and soon it will be dark.
Oh, where are they now, the tuneful tongues of affirmation,
the lovely limbs of play, the brown and gentle eyes that watched
me self-transcend?
This winter is too much; I do not need it.
My broken life bears fearful scars of twilight madness.
There is no comfort here.
Only hindsight carries suffering's secrets.
For pain is pain and death is death.
In darkness small and closed I want to be. I must retrace my
steps. There still is time. This moment's shame can be
outlived. Those foolish dreams were made for fools,
and only fools will try to make them true.

But wait! My water-love is calling now, so faint at first, but
warming once again my frightened soul: "Fear not; let go; trust
in our love. Surrender now and fight no more a war of false and
fruitless sacrifice. We have a bond, a green alluring secret. In me
you're new. All things are now within your reach because we're

one. And one with One who quickens all, incarnate "yes," his
name, "I Am."

So breathe in deeply now my special love and sink in me.
Come fill my heart, and precious be—
yet you be you, distinct from me."
And then I knew that in this liquid land of mystery
'twas Love herself I would embrace, and lose and find myself
in her . . .

Still on the board, alone and high, my confidence returns.
Those words of warmth have thawed the chill and brought the
light. Calling it by name I make the darkness mine.
And deep within, a strength so strange begins to move in me.
"In the desert of the heart
let the healing fountain start.
So jump, dive in, let go, let be;
explore the other side of me.
Commit, abandon, trust in me;
the other side of fear is free."

And pouring in, the power came. I still believe it was a time
of consecration.
My former graveyard-steps were measured new.
I hit the board and lifting, flew.
The point of pain was joy so full
and I was free.
Pulsed with powers from mountains and from oceans,
the dark nights of rocking pain eastered me into the high
places of ecstasy
I never knew before.

3. The Entry and the Third Window of Healing

Empty, receptive and very vulnerable,
I rose in timeless silence and easy energy.

Here was a new and riskful moment of commitment
—the first and frightening letting go . . .
But my faithful heart kept beating
and my loving lungs kept filling
and my blessed blood kept flowing.
For a Camelot-moment I was in ecstasy.
There was no compulsion here, no edgy expectation,
no two-tiered thinking.
In one split-moment I was truly me
yet truly all.
To be redeemed! Is this the final meaning?
—to be lost and found together,
to be one and all forever.

And so it was, that on that dark-brown day
I fell into the world.
And what a fall it was! More like the thrust of love.
Swift clean and true I entered in
and knew again the promised land that draws my life
forever now in time and tune together.
And so I knew my trust was true.
In but the time of holding-breath I lived a heaven.
My letting go was filled with harvest,
of heavy juice and hanging ripeness.
Embraced, consoled, I swayed and stayed in full abandon.
Like free-fall flight my way of being was reached
into another realm.
How good it was; how very good . . . dark
nights of tears were faint-remembered shadows
from another place. "Don't cling," the water said,
"just let me love." Don't rush or panic now,
be gentle with yourself. And ride your vision
through the scattered ghosts of doubt
like an eagle into dawn, a seed into the ground,

like knowledge into mystery.

'Twas on this emerald morning,
in the water-land of forgiveness,
I knew, in sorrow quick and seconds slow,
that from this place of love I must depart.
Full as I was of my new name and voice,
full too was I of clear
vocation.
Within the depths there was a call
—to *be* the love
—to *be* the mystery.
And so I knew I must return
but now her life and love were beating time in tune with mine.
There was no violence here
no words of exhortation, yet I knew
this was the last beginning.
And when this giant stretch of soul had happened
we laughed and laughed
because we understood
that I would never know the
water.

4. *The Reemergence and the Fourth Window of Change*

No lines no more, or black and white alone.
And colors new now blessed my eyes
and music round rinsed out my ears.
There was a lightness and a power. It was a time of
passion and of peace. A time of play, unfolding,
to a timeless timing in another space.
My dive, you see, was but a rite of passage . . .

The gloves from hands had fallen, and shoes from feet;
and wax from ears and scales from eyes.
But most of all, the sadness left the spirit

Spreading like a chestnut tree this universal
playground would be safe and held in trust,
its doors of welcome colored green.
As sunshine splits the mists, the gentle touch
of pure compassion
will spring the lock of mighty, muted power
held captive in the hearts of margin-souls
—the bonding gift of children,
the vision sure of women,
the wisdom of old age,
the challenge of the different,
the blessedness of the anawim,
the pent-up passion of a fettered world.
There would, of course, be conflict,
but conflict is a challenge for
divine imagination.
The battle sharp would rage till sunset in our souls,
then God would once again be free to be
a god for us.

The water now was urgent. I must come out.
So out I came and still remained. And thus forever,
leaving but remaining I would be
a paradox of beauty and of pain.
Below that purple nightfall
the boy became a man, the man became
the child divine.
The forests rang with wild delight beneath the humming moon
and small birds deep in love with shooting stars
gave up the chase, worn out with trying

to head them off and catch
their sworn light.

And so to work the vision.
A lifetime's false pursuits give way to issues real.
When half-gods go, the gods arrive in deep disguise.
The task is great—to change the world;
a cosmic transformation very soon.
But we have bread galore and wine aplenty
and multicolored hearts quite crazy
with a madness straight from God.
Oh, we will wander long through lands so strange
and many seasons. There will be dragons fierce and bluebirds
too and great wise fish in magic, stormy water.
. . . and every now and then another dancing dive which
    like first
Eden love goes on
forever.

NOTES

FIRST WINDOW

1. Carlos Valles, *Unencumbered by Baggage* (Gujarat Sahitya Prakash, 1987), p. 20 (words of de Mello).

2. Susan Griffin, *Woman and Nature: The Roaring Inside Her* (Harper and Row, 1978), p. 190.

3. Matthew Fox, *Original Blessing* (Bear and Co., 1983), p. 72.

4. John Briunin (ed.), *A Casebook on Dylan Thomas*, quoted in Matthew Fox, op. cit., p. 35.

5. Thomas Berry, interview article in *The Catholic Worker*, April 1989.

6. Monica Furlong, *Travelling In*, quoted in Circles of Experience (YMCA, 1985), p. 12.

7. Edward Robinson, *The Original Vision* (Religious Experience Research Unit, 1977), p. 50.

8. Kahlil Gibran, *The Prophet* (Alfred A. Knopf, 1977), p. 84.

9. Marsha Sinetar, *Do What you Love, the Money will Follow* (Paulist Press, 1987), p. 22.

10. Ibid. p. 29.

11. Mark Doughty, "Our Astonishing Universe," art. in *The Tablet* October 1988, p. 1242.

12. Sidney Simon, *Getting Unstuck* (Warner Books, 1988), p. 82.

13. Article, "Trends in Job Satisfaction," *San Francisco Chronicle*, April 12, 1989.

14. Eugene Kennedy, *A Time for Love* (Image Books, 1987), p. 141.

15. Horace Gregory (compiler), *e.e. cummings: a selection of poems* (Harcourt Brace Jovanovich, 1965), p. 88.

16. Viktor Frankl, quoted in Alan McGinnis, *The Friendship Factor* (Augsburg Publishing House, 1979), p. 96.

17. Dylan Thomas, from the poem "Fern Hill" in any of his Collected Works.

18. Brian Swimme, *The Universe Is a Green Dragon* (Bear and Co., 1984), see Part I.

SECOND WINDOW

1. Sheila Clarke, *Sharing the Darkness: The Spirituality of Caring* (Darton, Longman and Todd, 1988), p. 99.

2. Anthony de Mello, *One Minute Wisdom* (Doubleday, 1985), p. 58.

3. Daniel O'Leary, *A Way of Praying* (C.T.S., 1986), p. 13.

4. Richard Wilhelm (trans.), *The Secret of the Golden Flower*, quoted in Fox, op. cit., p. 138.

5. Eugene Kennedy, op. cit., p. 88.

6. Matthew Fox, *The Coming of the Cosmic Christ* (Harper and Row, 1988), p. 11.

7. T.C. McLuhan (compiler), *Touch the Earth* (Sphere Books, 1973), p. 6.

8. Ibid., p. 25.

9. Sam Keen, *The Passionate Life* (Harper and Row, 1983), p. 247.

10. Marilyn Ferguson, *The Aquarian Conspiracy* (Paladin, 1980), p. 430.

11. Marsha Sinetar, op. cit., p. 83.

12. Andrew Greeley, *Life for a Wanderer* (Image Books, 1969), p. 93.

13. Carlos Valles, op. cit., p. 95.

14. Matthew Fox (1988), p. 221.

15. Ibid.

THIRD WINDOW

1. Matthew Fox (1983), p. 185.

2. Ibid., p. 186.

3. Prov 8:22–23. 30–31.

4. Matthew Fox (1988), p. 62.

5. Willis Harman and Howard Rheingold, *Higher Creativity* (Jeremy P. Tarcher, Inc., 1984), p. 221.

6. Ibid., p. 25.

7. Ibid., p. 49.

8. Ibid., p. 6.

9. Matthew Fox (1988), p. 34.

10. T.S. Eliot, *The Four Quartets,* quoted in *New Review,* Vol. 2, No. 2 (editorial).

11. Karl Rahner, "Secular Life and the Sacraments," Part One, in *The Tablet,* Vol. 225, No. 6822 (March 1971), p. 237.

12. Daniel O'Leary, op. cit., p. 6.

13. Andrew Greeley, op. cit., p. 37.

14. Eugene Kennedy, op. cit., p. 132.

15. Anthony de Mello, op. cit., p. 111.

16. Matthew Fox (1983), p. 81.

FOURTH WINDOW

1. Matthew Fox, *A Spirituality Named Compassion* (Harper and Row, 1979), p. 17.

2. Ibid., p. 19.

3. Carlos Valles, op. cit., p. 94.

4. Matthew Fox, (1979), p. 33.

5. Ibid., p. 89.

6. Henri J.M. Nouwen, *Circles of Love* (Darton, Longman and Todd, 1988), p. 39.

7. Morris West, *Clowns of God* (Harcourt, Brace, Jovanovich, 1983), p. 396.

8. Henri J.M. Nouwen, *The Road to Daybreak* (Doubleday, 1988), p. 19.

9. David Spangler, *Emergence: The Rebirth of the Sacred* (Dell Publishing, 1984), p. 115.

10. Marsha Sinetar, op. cit., p. 116.

11. Anthony de Mello (1986), p. 12.

12. James Stephens, quoted in *New Review* (Spring 1984), p. 2.

13. Eugene Kennedy, op. cit., pp. 27–28.

14. Article, "The Shrinking World," in *Bottom Line Research*, Vol. 10, No. 3 (February 1989).

15. Guy Murchie, op. cit., p. 649.

16. Ibid.

17. T.C. McLuhan, op. cit., p. 54.

18. Marilyn Ferguson, op. cit., p. 418.

19. Joseph Campbell (with Bill Moyers), *The Power of Myth* (Doubleday, 1988), p. 22.

20. Dorothee Soelle, *To Work and To Love: A Theology of Creation* (Fortress Press, 1984), p. 137.

21. James B. Nelson, *Embodiment: An Approach to Sexuality, and Christian Theology* (Augsburg Publishing House, 1978), p. 18.

22. Dorothee Soelle, op. cit., p. 134.

23. Matthew Fox (1988), pp. 166-167.

24. Daniel O'Leary, *Year of the Heart* (Paulist Press, 1989).

25. Jolande Jacobi and R.F.C. Hull (eds.), *C.G. Jung: Psychological Reflections* (Princeton University Press, 1978), p. 105.